ANTS

ANTS

NIKITA CHINAMANTHUR

NEW DEGREE PRESS

COPYRIGHT © 2020 NIKITA CHINAMANTHUR

All rights reserved.

ANTS

ISBN   978-1-63676-615-7   *Paperback*
          978-1-63676-286-9   *Kindle Ebook*
          978-1-63676-287-6   *Ebook*

The Author has decided to use "experimental fiction" in this book which does not abide by the usual copy editing rules.

To all the ants in my life who still support me while doing a conga line around the coffee-table, even if I have swiped at them several times: I write because I know you will read.

CONTENTS

ACKNOWLEDGMENTS 11

PART 1. **HOMECOMING** **15**
CHAPTER 1. DISPLACEMENT 17
CHAPTER 2. VALENTINE'S DAY 23
CHAPTER 3. YELLOW 31
CHAPTER 4. HEY 37
CHAPTER 5. THE CHATROOM (MEETING PLACE) 41
CHAPTER 6. 18/7/18 45
CHAPTER 7. BUTTERFLIES ARE... 49
CHAPTER 8. TOMBOY 53
CHAPTER 9. WHOLE FOODS 61
CHAPTER 10. WHAT IF? 65

PART 2. **LOVE AT FIRST SEXT** **69**
CHAPTER 11. ARUNDHATI-VASISHTHA 71
CHAPTER 12. ASL 79
CHAPTER 13. CITY OF STARS 83
CHAPTER 14. BEN 89
CHAPTER 15. "FRIENDS DON'T TREAT EACH
OTHER LIKE SHIT." 93
CHAPTER 16. BITTERSWEET SYMPHONY 99
CHAPTER 17. "DON'T LET ANYONE CONVINCE
YOU THAT PLEASURE IS A SIN." 101
CHAPTER 18. NUMB 107
CHAPTER 19. FEET 111
CHAPTER 20. BLACK 113

PART 3. **FANTASIE** **117**

CHAPTER 21. INSOMNIA 119

CHAPTER 22. NAT / BEN 125

CHAPTER 23. HEAVEN OR LAS VEGAS 129

CHAPTER 24. GLASS 133

CHAPTER 25. I OWN MYSELF 137

CHAPTER 26. HER 141

CHAPTER 27. HIM 149

CHAPTER 28. NAT // BEN 153

CHAPTER 29. I AM NOT A PERSON 159

CHAPTER 30. IMY 163

PART 4. **BOMBAYWALLA** **171**

CHAPTER 31. BOREDOM 173

CHAPTER 32. MODESTY 179

CHAPTER 33. UNSETTLED 183

CHAPTER 34. NOT REALLY INDIAN 187

CHAPTER 35. OMAR 191

CHAPTER 36. DAKSHINA 195

CHAPTER 37. BREAK KE BAAD 199

CHAPTER 38. TAILSPIN 205

CHAPTER 39. RUMI 209

CHAPTER 40. LOVE 219

PART 5. **RESIDUE** **225**

CHAPTER 41. WYD 227

CHAPTER 42. ANNIVERSARY 231

CHAPTER 43. 19/12/19 235

CHAPTER 44. TRAUMA 239

CHAPTER 45. DUST 243

CHAPTER 46. RO(MAN)CE 251

CHAPTER 47. S(HE) SAID 255

CHAPTER 48. REINVENTION   259

CHAPTER 49. REGRET HANGOVER   263

CHAPTER 50. ANTH   273

AFTERWORD   283

APPENDIX   291

ACKNOWLEDGMENTS

We made it! A year in the making, a lifetime of storytelling, and I have published my first book. I've got loads of people to thank but I'd like to highlight a few:

- To Rachel Minseo Koo—without whom *Ants* would never exist—thank you for being my rock. I couldn't have done this without your support or your belief in this book.
- To Mummy and Daddy—I wouldn't be here without either of you—thank you for being an amazing set of parents, and friends.
- To the extended Chi(n)nama(n)t(h)ur-Dabir-Kappago-mtula-Vangala clans—in alphabetical order so as to not incite any in-fighting.
  - To the cousins I can't bear to spend the holidays without: I'm grateful to have spent Christmas 2019 with **every** one of you.
  - To the long list of *thathas, ajjis,* and my one and only *ammama*: thank you for raising me and my parents. Thank you for the *dosas, puris,* and stories.
  - To the great-grandmothers (*nayanamma, gillu-gillu muthavva, ajji-bajji,* Sundari *ajji*) who have imparted

such awe-inspiring wisdom: I hope I will continue to do justice to your memories and legacies.

- To my lovely Fawks (AA, BB, HB, RK, JL, MM, IR)— thank you for tolerating my constant influx of memes. Let us never stop spilling the tea.
- To the teachers, professors, and educators who mentored me into becoming the student and person I am today from Small World to Scripps. Thank you for introducing me to all the literary heroes I aspire to be. To IS—for giving me a lifetime of memories (and stressors) to unpack in therapy—I love you and your silly idiosyncrasies.

To my beta readers, I hope you enjoy this version more than you enjoyed the first one, typos and all. Thank you for giving your honest and thorough feedback over the course of three weeks as I rushed to meet my copy-editing deadline:

- Andrea Tang
- Aditi Garg
- Amy Kouch
- Janica Mendillo
- Anita Shekar
- Becca Mamlet

To Eric Koester, Rob Alston, Sarah Lobrot, Brian Bies, and the entire creative team at New Degree Press and the Creator Institute. Eric, thank you for reaching out in July 2019 and the rest of the Creator Institute for being so accommodating. Rob, thank you for bearing with me throughout the first part of my journey. Sarah, I can't thank you enough for all your help, support, and our hour-long, time-difference-impacted calls.

Lastly, to all those I could not mention, thank you for liking, sharing, commenting, following, and supporting me throughout this journey.

PART I

HOMECOMING

DISPLACEMENT

CALIFORNIA, 19 DECEMBER 2019

Three suitcases cast long shadows over her small, seated body. One massive, towering structure contained all the memories and non-memories of college. Her Bluetooth speakers. Her recently acquired American flag. Her childhood stuffed animals. All packed neatly into a thirty-liter hard-backed suitcase and two smaller, carry-on-sized bags. One, a gift with a spectacular abstract pattern, the other a simple blue one with her father's name scrawled all over it. The 'i' and 'r' had smeared off over the years, and all that remained was a hastily scribbled "V k am" in her mum's pen. Her last name was all over the dented back in several colors: black, red, silver, green, every color but the color of the suitcase itself.

It was a blisteringly sunny, yet pleasant, southern California morning. Cold enough to warrant a sweatshirt, bright enough for sunglasses. Nat didn't know if it was a California thing or just a warm weather thing, but Cali weather had this amazing ability to make her feel absolutely freezing and way too overdressed at the same time. She could feel the sweat seep through her sweatshirt but felt appeased by the overpowering smell of Chanel's *Mademoiselle*. It was her grown-up perfume, ironic since *mademoiselle* means "young lady" in French. It was the same four-year old bottle her dad had brought back from his trip to India; duty-free in Dubai is any desi's dream. That and maybe shopping in Canada where the dollar can stretch twenty-five percent further.

Even in thick denim, Nat could feel the asphalt scratching her thighs as she uncomfortably shifted her weight onto her behind. She checked her phone, darkened through her sunglasses' lenses, to see her Uber's status. Perched on the edge of the sidewalk, she craned her neck to catch a glimpse of the passing car's license plate. *7Z4, nope.* She sighed, and let her foot make invisible circles in the concrete as she waited for her ride. Her Aviators hid her bloodshot, sleepless eyes from pedestrians who barely paid her any attention. She wore her over-the-ear headphones, listening to her 2020 playlist. The one she had made for the year that had yet to arrive. It was filled with nostalgia in the shape of the Red Hot Chili Peppers and other overrated 90s alternative hits from the likes of The Offspring and Sublime.

Mindlessly, she swiped back to her messages and saw the last one Rumi had sent her. A quick one-liner about some interesting guest lecturer in her philosophy class. Nat fought the urge to text back, but relented and tapped out a lengthy, rambling note about her trip to India. And, her indecision to leave school. And, how shitty her last final had been. Nat missed her friend terribly. At one point, Rumi was the only person who could contact Nat at any time of the day. Nat had stopped responding to her parents for a hot minute, and Rumi was the one who had metaphorically walked her away from the ledge. Eight weeks later and Nat was planning on spending nearly a year with her parents, hoping to reconcile her relationship with them. And, with herself.

What Nat didn't know was the lengths it would take for her to reach a spiritual, emotional, and mental equilibrium.

In half an hour, Nat would leave her college's vast campus. Leave for good in many ways. In any case, she would not return as the same Nat.

In an hour, Nat would be on a California interstate, whizzing down the road doing eighty-five on a sparse lane, in a stinking Prius with stained interior seats and a caking of grime on the exterior. California dust, desert dust that got everywhere imaginable.

In two hours, Nat would have a breakdown in the airport, surrounded by strangers. She would heave and heave until her chest stopped racking with sobs. She would then phone her parents, who would try to console and calm her down while breaking in and out due to the spotty reception.

"Not now, *beta*," they would urge. "Wait, until we get there… Until we can see you. Just—just make sure you don't miss the flight."

In four hours, Nat would be on a plane, headed in the wrong direction, going all the way around the world to reach her final destination. A massive, meticulously planned vacation, touring all of North India from the Thar Desert to the Himalayas to an Assamese tea estate. Vikram, her father, wanted one last hurrah before starting her four-month self-imposed sabbatical. It was their first big family trip since she had started college, and the only traveling she would be doing before returning in the fall. Her homecoming in India would last over a month. Of course, they had to make the obligatory trip down south to Bangalore. She would spend time shopping in busy Christmastime crowds, hours riding in a boat of a van, taking pictures of her grandparents and their houses and their habits and their lives. Documenting, journaling, scrapbooking. She would pester and make them pose in lines, in front of the framed photographs of her great-grand-parents. Her *Ajji's veena*. Her *Ammama's vankaaya*. Her *doctor-thatha's* spectacles. Her *Major-thatha's* essaying notebook.

All reminders of home, her first home.

In six weeks, Nat would be home. Her real home in the US. The one with her yellow-tinted bedroom and blue walls. Red brick, and wood paneling. She'd open the door to her bedroom, smelling its ripeness, its disuse. And, notice how more wood was peeling off the doorframe. How it was splintering and breaking. She'd frown and worry about hurting her bare feet. She'd switch on the bathroom light, and her eyes would be drawn to the mold on the ceiling. The dripping tap. The decaying vanity mirror. The caked soap on the dispenser spout. She'd notice a couple small ants scurrying around the gray, woven bathroom mats, and a much bigger one leading the way.

She'd notice how the ants would run towards the water, instead of away. Almost deliberately ending their lives prematurely. She would observe as they ran back and forth, and she'd hesitate for a millisecond before swiping them away. The metallic scent of their death, their blood, invading her nostrils and creasing her nose. Nat would rinse her hands, while making tired eye-contact with herself in the mirror. Home.

She'd see her restless eyes, bloodshot from the lack of sleep and jet lag, darkly encircled eyes from the long nights and early mornings. She'd feel the dryness of her fingertips as she scrubbed her hands with soap. The memory of her summer flooding back with the scent of the soap: lavender. She'd reel and feel her heart lurch for California in a way it hadn't before. She would miss a place she had run away from only a few months ago. Nat would put away the soap and use the one that didn't smell as potent.

She would breathe in the crisp outside air, freshly snowed air, feeling her allergy symptoms disappear. She would sit quietly in her backyard, legs crossed, arms pressed against her sides. Warm but not comfortable. She would want to *feel* Washington again. She would want to remember what it was like running in the switchbacks or feeling the wet turf on her shoes or the mud on the field. The weight of her rain jacket, and the heaviness in her head after a run. She would want to remember what it was being a kid again, even if she had never really lived as a kid. A childhood marred by academia and ambition rather than play and frivolity. Her privilege, she knew, she fucking *knew* too deeply to ever express those feelings of resentment to her parents. She never lived like a child because she didn't know what that meant. Running outside, walking to the corner shop and buying ice cream, swimming in the community pool, drawing with chalk on the road, the chasteness of a first kiss.

Nat would, with a guffaw, go back inside her home. Her house with the flat roof and low ceilings. Sky blue walls, and wooden floors. She'd laugh at her dad's joke, and help her mum make dinner. She'd ignore the anxiety, the one that had haunted her every night in her college dorm. Permeating through her laptop and her unfinished novels and her to-do lists. Her lack of productivity as defined in a capitalist society. Her lack of productivity that directly correlated with her lack of purpose or importance. Because she didn't do anything, she didn't count.

Nat would not anticipate falling in love or being content. She wouldn't expect meeting someone so soon after leaving college. She wouldn't expect the restless nights, full of Frank Ocean and The Weeknd. She wouldn't expect the bated breaths with which she waited impatiently for his next message. She wouldn't have imagined feeling sexy again. She wouldn't have dreamt of the things she would do to prove her love for him.

I

VALENTINE'S DAY

———

WASHINGTON, 14 FEBRUARY 2020

It wasn't a good cry.

What had started as an innocent grocery list for her father ended in a few chest-heaving sobs. She pressed her cool fingers under her eyes, attempting to fight off any indication she had wept. It was over in less than a few minutes, and she jumped out of her comfortable cocoon of blankets to wash her face. Her eyes hardly registered the mess of old clothes, ones that didn't fit her anymore, heaped on top of her dresser and the spider scuttling on the floor. Instead, she forced herself to confront the sink in front of her. Leaning in over the edge as far as she could on tiptoes without wetting her shirt, she started washing her hands. She had changed the placement of one of her rings so it sat snugly on her middle finger, instead of her left ring finger. She hadn't gotten used to the feeling or the appearance of the ring on that finger. The *engagement* finger. *God, how I wish I were a little closer to being engaged sometimes.* She stared morosely at the mirror's peeling veneer frame and hastened washing her hands. *Fuck, I really thought this Valentine's Day would be kinda good.* Splashing her face with some water and drying off with a towel, she slunk back towards her bed. Inhaling deeply but with some difficulty, she buried herself under her sheets again and found the tiniest bit of solace in another faceless, nameless conversation.

Sometimes, she thought cynically as she replied, *it's better to drown in someone else's problems.*

In the past week, Natasha had turned down no less than eight offers to "hang out and cuddle" or "smoke." Two of these messengers were determined to meet her in person, aggressively suggesting a time and place. The objective of this meeting…? Losing her virginity.

She rolled her eyes as she scrolled through the messages and sighed, tapping back to Instagram. She scrolled over meme after meme. TikTok after TikTok. She finally gained the encouragement to restart her playlist, basking in the anguished sounds of angry West Coast rap and bedroom indie. She let her mind wander slightly, jerking back to alertness when noticing the clock. She'd have to start getting ready soon. A decade of living in her parents' home made her comfortable with traffic fluctuations and the time needed to get to wherever she needed to be. Nat hadn't gone out for herself in a while, only for those daily workouts.

Over a month, she thought, *since I've had any significant alone time away from the parents.*

She had disappeared at 9:35 p.m. last Wednesday night to watch a film, feeling an eerie sense of unease walking through a brightly lit, nearly deserted mall and cinema bathroom. It was midnight by the time she had gotten back into her car to return home.

Then, a mini-reunion with Rumi on Thursday. That was the busiest she'd been in at least a month. Rumi had taken a bus all the way north to Washington from college for a weekend. It was a spontaneous, impulsive, resolutely teenage decision. Nat and her best friend had barely exchanged a few words before Rumi excitedly interjected some boring comment.

"Guess what, N?!" Rumi's chirpiness, even through the phone, brought a jarringly fresh vibe into Nat's musty bedroom. She hadn't changed the sheets since she had flown back from India.

"What?" Nat wasn't really feeling it at the time. Fresh off a wave of despondency and melancholia, she fidgeted with a fraying edge of her phone's case and stared with glassy-eyed intensity at the LED screen. Her eyes were already hurting from crying *and* staying up too late last night.

"I'm coming home!" Rumi rushed. "Well, not home, really. Just for the weekend! Min Seo is going to meet her friend in Huntington Beach, and I figured if *she* could bus south, I *could* come up for a little bit. I don't have classes on Monday, because of—"

Nat barely heard Rumi after that short conversation. She didn't know how to explain her *situation,* or condition, to her best friend. She watched as Rumi was interrupted by Min Seo and feigned interest at their conversation and inside jokes; her heart swelled with jealousy, and she swallowed a lump in her throat. *Would anything ever go back to… normal?*

"So… what do you think?"

Nat cleared her throat and grinned. "Honestly, I can't wait. Let's spend as much time as you can spare, okay?! I've missed you a lot!" Nat felt the glare of tears and coughed to hide it a little bit. Rumi watched her intensely through the screen.

Even with all the cheerfulness and peer-mentor-positivity, Rumi had fought her own demons and recognized some of them haunting Nat. Maybe too many of them.

"Are you sure you're okay?"

"I'm home, Ru. At least I'm home." Nat spoke softly. "If I were back at my dorm, I think I would just... break."

Rumi nodded thoughtfully and set her phone down meaningfully on her desk. She leaned in, urging Nat to go on.

"It's okay, dude. I can't cry anymore." Nat chuckled weakly and sighed. "I've been trying my hand at... uh... the online thing again..." She ended sheepishly, looking suggestively at Rumi. "And, this one guy was hella, and I mean hella, ripped."

"Oooh, spill!"

They launched into an excitable, hour-long, meaningless conversation about a random stranger Nat had barely met.

Nat ended up riding the wave of euphoric social interaction and broke a few of her rules that weekend. She flirted with a few more random people on **The Chatroom.** Then she sent them close-up pictures of her tits and pretended they weren't hiding in some stranger's phone. Things were going alright until she felt a crash in her energy and her mood. She was displeased and distant. Nat didn't feel like she was truly affecting any change in her life. This kind of dissatisfaction forced her to look for pleasure through anonymity and flirty banter. Honestly, she didn't want to linger on those emotions too long.

Of course, she *had* played the same songs since January, and it cast a repetitive pathology to her movements. Wake up to Frank Ocean, eat to the penultimate season of *The Good Place*, and sleep to The Weeknd's crooning. *At least I'm not getting any spam messages from the bots of phishing cam-sites,* she snorted.

Here she lay, nearly twenty, very lonely, and hopeful. Hopeful that something would change within her if she gave her body a chance. Hopeful that when she returned to college, she would feel different and act differently. Maybe she'd try chugging and shots… maybe. Loosen up, find some friends.

It took her the course of a few years to realize if anyone was her partner, it was her phone. She lived, breathed, and slept online. The internet was her most trusted adviser and the revealer of most of her secrets. She'd guarded them so closely for a while that her sudden decision to release them into the nether didn't go unnoticed by her psyche. The growing pit in her stomach disappeared for those few euphoric seconds after she pressed send on a risky text, or worse, a lewd picture. She'd bite her lip, squeeze her eyes shut, and formulate the next way to tell the world about her desires, her shames, and her compromises.

Maybe, she'd feel more accountable or more accepted if they validated her desires, and her body parts. Signed off like a parking ticket or a timecard. Maybe a heart-eyes or drool emoji would do the trick. Hundreds and hundreds of straight white men who liked to call her "exotic," and even once "chocolate goddess." Even though Nat herself resembled something more of a yellow, pimply beige. She *wished* she could be a "chocolate goddess."

She was short and fat. Check.

She was funny and flirty. Check and check.

She hadn't ever touched another human besides through a fiber optic connection.

Definite, solid blue check.

Then there were the things she couldn't put into words. The music she listened to and what it made her feel (Indian love songs from her childhood, and remorseful about her lost

desi self). The simulation she craved and what she did without it (masturbate). The people she'd never met but missed
(mindlessly scroll through Instagram, double-tapping on pictures of college celebrities; like the one with cute Southwest-
ern-inspired earrings, and the other with a constant influx
of golden-hour selfies). Her insecurities and body negativity
(never look at a mirror).

The confidence she had gained over the years. Her presence in any classroom. Her thoughtful insights about Chau-
cer and Hurston. Her penchant for the iambic pentameter
and aptitude for Middle English texts. The way her tongue
and lips would curl and roll to say "k-nee-gh-tuh" and "tray-
wuh-ly" instead of knight or truly. Her succinct analyses of
Janie's own self-determination, and the obvious similarities
in both their stories.

Nat, like Hurston's Janie, wanted to be a blossoming
cherry tree; instead, she stayed a squat prune tree, sour and
astringent. The snark and snarl, one of which had withered
away during her year-and-a-half of college. Her biting desire
to relax and to reach for those things that were less than an
arm's length away from here.

She was ashamed she didn't have the ambition or drive
she had had at sixteen. She was ashamed that in less than
a few years she had gained nearly double the weight she
gained over a decade. She ruminated on the books that had
made her reassess her place in the world: *American Psycho*,
Middlesex, and now *The Girl with the Dragon Tattoo*. She
resented her affinity to Pat Bateman, a cruel reminder that
her name rhymed with his as did some of his insanities. Her
twirling, dynamic sexuality as it was challenged every time
she read about Cal (née Calliope). Nat lusted after Lisbeth's
strength, her independence. And, the rate at which Lis could

eat white-bread sandwiches. Characters whose depth and anguish she empathized with, even if she hadn't experienced a third of their struggles. Pain is relative, in any case.

She noticed the small graceful attributes she'd acquired over the years chatting up strangers on the internet. Her easy banter and gratuitous flourishes. Her fingernails sounding like Morse code as she tapped on her phone screen vigorously, if not akin to a difficult rhythm section.

She felt exposed to all the pollution she'd never seen. The covert sexism, the griminess of seeking sex online, the red lights. She admired her forearms instead of her torso, feeling the blatant need to justify the emotion with disgust over her rounded belly and jiggly thighs. She forced herself to stop analyzing herself with a male gaze or the gaze of a sexual partner.

She couldn't.

She *just* wasn't her type.

Instead, she grit her teeth and continued to brush. She thought about how she had spilt her guts to Rumi who, as well-intentioned as she may be, was distracted and told her about her class schedule. She watched as Rumi giggled with Min Seo, her new roommate and Nat's spiritual replacement, and felt her best friend slipping past with an unrecognized urgency. Nat wanted to end the call then. She didn't feel good and definitely didn't think she looked good enough to be introduced to several people over a nauseating video chat. Spitting in the sink a few times, she checked her face and quickly rinsed it. Patting it down, she made a note of the time.

II

YELLOW

Two hours later, Nat was back in her bedroom with the yellow walls, after a gut-wrenchingly long workout. She placed her keys on the dresser, a bad habit she had picked up from dorm life. And, stripped before entering the shower once she had picked a song from her newest Hindi playlist.

It was another cold day in February, the sunlight barely streaming through her blinds. If the blinds were kept open, the light would bounce off the pale-yellow walls and flood her room with sparkling dust particles. Blinds closed, the room was still oddly sunny. Bright but cold. The air felt thin, lackluster.

This was her sanctuary. This was where, half-buried in her Harry Potter sheets, she would message back and forth with dozens of men. This was where Nat dreamt, reimagined, speculated, fantasized.

Her bedroom had always been sparsely furnished. A large, queen-sized bed placed under the high window. It was low, and the top of her mattress reached her mid-calf. Her comforter-*du-jour* was an old Harry Potter themed extravaganza, with weirdly stretched cottony faces of the Golden Trio. A long, bright purple—because she had selected it when she was thirteen—dresser on the opposite wall, next to *her* bathroom. The sink was free-standing, in front of the only exposed red-brick wall in their house. Either a fashionable choice from the mid-eighties or just a clumsy handyman's work, she had no idea. Being an only child has some perks, bathroom included.

Wrapping her wet hair in a towel and occasionally sneezing, Nat sat on her bed, painstakingly moisturizing and listening to the *Rockstar* album. Humming mindlessly along with AR Rahman's voice, she got back under her covers even though it was barely 5 p.m. She spent all day propped up with her head against the wall and one leg dangling off the edge and onto the floor. Buried in a book, or doodling, or on her phone.

Okay, it was always her phone. She scrolled through the dozens of Valentine's Day posts, rolling her eyes, and biting the inside of her cheek in frustration.

She thought about all the bubbles she'd lived in: this bedroom, this house, this neighborhood, her high school, this city. And then her college.

Sheltered, unchanging, possessive bubbles that sucked her in and left her to suffocate rather than be led astray.

The air in the bedroom was so cold now, she could barely leave her bed without her fingers immediately freezing in position, brittle, nearly on the verge of shattering. The cold had penetrated her entire body, apart from one thing. While her metaphorical baby-oven stayed nicely protected, with 24/7 heating, the layers of fat on her stomach became of some use. They shielded her belly from the air and let her exposed arms and face and nose deal with the chill.

She sunk deeper into her sheets and pulled them up over her head. *Why is it so cold?!* She wasn't sure sometimes if she was imagining the temperature. It was so volatile, so, so cold. Still scrolling, Nat groaned and shut her phone off angrily. Before switching it back on resignedly and switching apps. *I wonder who's on* **The Chatroom** *right now.* She refreshed the page and noticed a snarky post that had been made ten seconds before. Smirking, she slowly exited her cocoon to sit up straight and take off her soaking towel. Running her hands through her hair, she direct-messaged the poster and swiped back to the main feed.

When she had stepped out of the room a few hours prior, and squinted at the skylight, heat flooded over her in a tsunami wave and she had realized, *no, the house was just too old to heat up properly.* She unnecessarily worried that someday soon she'd become too old to make love to properly. Appropriately. She worried she was suspended between two worlds, one online and the other surrounded by a protective mucus, trapped inside a bubble.

Natasha liked her bubbles though. They were oddly permeable like a cell wall, able to capture things from the outside that were meant to be on the inside, and transparent. She could see the outside world as much as she liked, pressing her nose to its membrane, reading about things halfway around the world. And, for her, the bubble spanned nine-thousand miles. All the way to Bangalore, to her family. She still could see in their eyes and hear in their ears and walk in their footsteps. It wasn't so distant; it never really was. Her bubble grew thinner each year, almost tempting her to pop it. Expose herself to the carbon dioxide in the atmosphere. She didn't though, as tempted as she was, because her aversion to risk seemed even more imposing. Her college bubble didn't exist anymore, it had been rudely burst by unkind strangers and hours of loneliness. So, she had just withered away in the unknown atmosphere, nearly suffocating.

College had ended so many good parts of her, the ones with confidence and *joie-de-vivre*. The ones where she didn't just obsess over boys. When she returned, she knew none of that would matter anyway. Keeping her head down, and her eyes on the clouds, she would be leaving the place as quickly as she had arrived. Bubble or not, she'd grit her teeth and work her ass off to succeed. That was the only option.

The phantom touch of another's thumb over her chin, warm arms over her goosebumps, a breath in her ear, a chin nuzzled in the back of her neck, feathery kisses over her non-existent clavicle and further down, a hand running through her hair gently, a mouth nipping at hers. All she could do that morning was dream. About a fake relationship, about a fake human who cared enough. About what she would do if she could leave the bed immediately every morning, or throw open the bedroom door widely, squinting, allowing the heat and sunlight to enter.

Instead, she watched with a cry stuck in her esophagus at the light that peeked beneath the wooden door, begging for entrance. Instead, she focused on her daydreams. A hollow laugh, a heartbeat, a casual hand on her waist. At that moment, she just felt incredibly alone. Impassive at the prospect, yet truly alone. She knew once her mum started unloading the dishwasher and turning on and turning off the kitchen faucet, the noise would distract her from her loneliness.

Until then, she had nothing to do but dream. Listen to the birds squawk. Think of a flowering cherry tree. A summer that was promised, and a winter that never seemed to end. Cloying into her bones and speckling her skin with goosebumps.

Before she went back to college, she wanted to cling onto some relic from her childhood. Something to make her feel like home, or to make her feel less lonely. Something real, something she could hold to her heart instead of holding in her sobs. Would it be her books? Or her memories? Or the scant number of photos in which she was featured with her friends? A running list of to-do lists and homework assignments? The drawers of papers, notes, classwork that she hung onto? Could she ever Marie Kondo her shit or not? Did they bring her joy or was she pretending?

Is it pretense if you don't know whether it's fake or real? Are humans able to understand the depth of their feelings? The accuracy? Or are we all weather forecasters, basing our observations on science, but really just by having faith in the system? I feel happy. Why do I doubt this is what happy feels like? And, when I feel sad, why is it crushing, abusive, turbulent? Why can't it be like happiness, just existing?

In the mornings, with enough sunlight, her blinds would block a golden stream of light from entering her room. The light stayed trapped between the folds of the curtains and blinds, attempting to insulate an uninsulated room. Yet, the light would still shine. Nothing could stop it from brightening up her entire room in the morning, through the trees, the blinds, and the curtains.

She resonated in the jarring reality of it. In some ways, a lot of ways, those bubbles had trapped the heat out of her spaces. And, while she could feel it against the membrane, it was lost to her. If she wanted that warmth, that heat, that phantom caress, she would have to burst the bubble. The thick, mucus-membraned one, basically a teenage amniotic sac that had sustained her from seven years old, and still existed after leaving her home. She felt the moment she'd burst it, a pungency would fill her nostrils. Force her to weather the stench for a few more years after it. As though that lingering smell would never truly leave her body. She'd always reek of inexperience and her naivety. And, while it would take a moment to do, it would also take years of getting used to living without its shelter, its protection. She didn't think she was ready. She didn't feel ready.

But, how could she depend on her feelings if there weren't any?

Her phone buzzed and she snapped out of her infinite scrolling (and never-ending stream of thoughts) to check the notification. That was how she lived, from one notification to the next. With a sideways grin, Nat started responding to this equally frustrated stranger.

6:18 PM, 2/14/2020

brattypatty is online
brattypatty is typing...
Yeah lmao everyone deserves to get laid on Valentine's Day
You got plans lol?

tanning.chatum is online
tanning.chatum is typing...
Hahah no
Cant really fw girls rn

Really?
Who broke your heart???

III

HEY

—

10:19 PM, 2/16/2020

tanning.chatum is online
tanning.chatum is typing…
Weve been chatting for like two days now
But you never told me your name

brattypatty is online
brattypatty is typing...
Oh, hi there lol

Heyyy
So what is it

What?

Your name

Um, guess lmao.
This has already been such a weird conversation.

Lol ok I feel you.
Ive never spoke to anyone about my kinks or porn
And I cant believe
Were into the same shit

Haha, I can't say I've never... but I get whatchu mean

Hm :)
You still haven't told me your name

You still haven't guessed!!!

Ok but at least give me a hint

Hm... first letter N. It's short lol

Uhh
Nini
Nuki
Naomi
Numi
Nora

Lmao what kind of name is Nuki???

Idkkkk just tell me already

Aight
I'll give you another hint

Ugh ok

First two letters are N and A.
Come on, you only have to guess a third 😂

Nam
Nak
Nai
Nag

Lmao wtffff

Wait I think I got it!!
Nar!!!

-facepalm-

What???? What is it?
Naj
Nad
Naf
Nar

Literally you said Nar before… omfg

Nat

Ding ding ding! Yeah, like Black Widow!

Wait seriously!!!
Wow Im so good at this
What Black Widow?

Like… Marvel? You know

Natasha Romanoff??? Black Widow???
There are literally thirty movies out???
How do you NOT know Black Widow???
C'mon dude.

Uh yeah idk who dat
Well, anyways
lol hi Nat

Hi :) wait…
idk your name tho…???

Guess bitch

IV

THE CHATROOM (MEETING PLACE)

———

They existed under the surface of every browser window, internet hole, and now a mobile application like **The Chatroom**.

An innocent chat button. Lurking behind a Contact Us section or on a subreddit. Nat found all her men online. She couldn't afford the rejection of regular dating apps or Snapchat streaks. A rejection in real life, with her real profile and connected Facebook, would sting too much to bear. Real life acknowledges the other person's humanity, and she couldn't care less about imagining a real person feeling real emotions about her. Because the moment those feelings soured, they could have tangible consequences. Online, there were no consequences. So, she relied on her steady supply of anonymous users, in incognito tabs and over VPN connections. She carefully extracted her personal information, readily available in usernames and handles, email addresses, and phone numbers, until her digital chat footprint was close to naught.

With the exception of pictures. *Her* pictures. Those were, of course, a new occurrence in her daily schedule. After chatting for a few hours, or a few minutes, she'd readily disperse her image onto their screens. It was a cold, calculated strategy to phish for compliments (pun intended, she never actually wanted to know who these people were in real life; that wasn't in her best interest). The validation would soothe her burns after not talking to guys for days, or weeks, or years. They were quick, easy fixes. A way to conquer her fears while liberating her most treasured self. Validation from strangers just tasted sweeter, even if she didn't believe it half of the time. Nat was no stranger to the web. In fact, she despised how much she had come to explore some of the oddest corners of the floating, available open internet: Reddit, Rabbit (now Kast), sometimes Craigslist and, rarely, 4Chan. Of course, there were also the download-free, registration-free chat rooms. And **The Chatroom**: *her* chatroom. People all over the world are lonely, and the internet is quick to provide them with weird, skeevy rabbit-holes to explore.

She knew if she ever took the step to download Tor and venture into the Dark Web, she would never be the same. Sex, legal and illegal, would be too readily available, as well as her digital fingerprints. Those would be smeared across each hyperlink, each click. Nat wanted anonymous encounters, not dangerous ones. Hell, even reading some (hopefully) fictional erotica, she had realized that there were more than a handful of truly demented people online. Nat wasn't one to kink-shame, but self-cannibalism? Or even more bizarre... consensual cannibalism? Viral internet sensation *Two Girls, One Cup* aside, scat and piss-play were its own weird categories. *I mean,* she grimaced, *people actually post themselves doing urine-cleanses on Instagram now and making cheese from breastmilk.* But eating human flesh was like two steps above vegetarianism, and she couldn't handle that. Tor would be a gateway into that. And, human sex trafficking, and rape porn. And, worse… child porn. The most vile things people are doing all available in a moment's notice. It was nauseating.

She valued her safety a lot, too much to meet anybody in person. *Him*, included. *Him*, especially. Because if *he* weren't the person *he* claimed to be, Nat knew that would break her completely. If *he* were actually a middle-aged woman in Nebraska, she'd probably have a fit and then just stop trusting people entirely. *As true Crime Junkies will tell you, you never really know someone.* Online was cleaner, and sweeter to taste. Anonymity is a mask that just turns up the anticipation, the exhilaration, the excitement.

Better even, Nat smirked, *if they like what you look like after you send them the nudes. Oooh, like that drunk guy from two weeks ago.*

On the other hand, she had no value for her privacy. Intrinsically, she knew her faith in the anonymous internet had worn out many, many years ago. There was no such thing as real anonymity online anymore. However, there was such a thing as overpopulation. Scores, multitudes, leagues of people scoured the internet today. Scrolling through apps, or downloading images and videos, or even uploading *certain* images and videos. No matter how many people she propagated *her* images to, there would always be too many images circulating to find hers intentionally.

A drop in an ocean.

A grain of sand in the desert.

Impossible to find.

V

18/7/18

———

FLIGHT FROM DUBAI TO SEATTLE, 18 JULY 2018

Jostling slowly behind my parents, I squeezed myself and the mini blue carry-on through the plane's aisle. I was exhausted for some reason, and my usual alert self was faltering. I yawned widely as we waited for someone to lift their suitcase into the overhead compartment. Before they struggled too much, my dad swooped in with a large, helpful smile and hoisted it up. My eyes followed the motion from the other aisle, and even through my exhaustion, I kept a sharp look out for any attractive people. You know, the kind of silly thing we do in an airport. Mind you, I would be in a window seat, separated from any strangers. There was no prospect of a meet-cute on a fourteen-hour flight. My hood was up, and with only a few thick strands of curly hair escaping through the opening, I was pretty much ready to crash once we reached our seats.

Dubai to Seattle. Our last, longest leg on our way back home. India was my grad trip, ha. While some of my other (former) classmates were traipsing across Europe or the

States, I had been forced to go back to India. I mean, not forced like dragged out of my bed or something. More like, I didn't know what I wanted to do during the summer before college started and here we were.

Before long, we reached our seats and I squeezed self-consciously into the space, taking off my backpack before I had to sit down. Pushing my backpack under the seat in front of me and feeling the warm air from the window, I latched my seatbelt and closed my eyes. I could feel my mum look me over once and shift a little bit to talk to my dad. The low murmur of voices was suddenly broken by a long, extended wail. A baby. Groaning quietly, I forced my eyes open. I was way too awake now.

"Hey, mama. Have you seen this movie?" I snuggled up against her and navigated through the Hindi movies on her screen.

She snorted. "Didn't you want to sleep?"

"No. That baby really woke me up."

"You're such a cartoon. Go back to sleep. This is a good time to."

I stifled a yawn and looked up at her. She was patting my arm soothingly, determined to lull me into sleep.

Surprisingly, I let her.

My dreams were hazy and vague. Full of exciting college experiences, like a massive house party, studying at the beautiful library, late-night introspective conversations about the meaning of life. And, maybe a little too much semi-anonymous sex. Silhouettes of co-eds jumping up and down loomed over the other images, laminated to form some type of wild Friday night.

A wild Friday night I expected to materialize in the fall. Two months, and I would be in college. *Fuck, dude.* It's almost as if I were being tantalized by my parents' amazing college days and the hundreds of movies about coming of age and growing up while at university.

This is what it's going to be like, the voice in my head leered as I shifted to a more comfortable position in my seat. I felt a sharp push against my headrest and was jerked out of my slumber again. Some kid behind me was playing a game on the screen, apparently. The lights had changed in the cabin to a purple haze—meaning it was night-time in the time-zone we were zipping past. I felt my stomach grumble, and I glanced down at my bulging sweatshirt, constricted by the belt. My tummy felt more restrained, and I gnawed at the inside of my cheek in annoyance and hunger.

You could have prevented this, you know. The voice was softer, more mocking now. *All you had to do was eat well and exercise.*

Uncomfortably shifting, I tried to think about something other than food. My gaze drifted to the dog-eared, second-hand copy of *Middlesex* in the seat back-pocket. Pulling it from the net, I started reading, focusing closely on each word, sentence, and paragraph. As I drifted between the story of a Turko-Greek family and my own hunger, I became more intrigued at the prospect of Cal's story. *Why*, I swallowed to ignore my stomach rumbling, *did this random, cisgender man write this book? And, what actually gave him the right to this story?*

Stifling a wide yawn, I pushed the book back into the seat-back pocket and settled back, feeling the belt dig into my stomach.

VI

BUTTERFLIES ARE...

———

Ryan. He once told me I turned a shade of magenta when I blushed. I've never seen it myself, as generally when I'm embarrassed, I don't immediately run to the bathroom to see the color of my cheeks. It was the weirdest thing a guy had said to me at that point in time. Apparently, like a chameleon, I changed into the color of my jacket, a big puffy purple beast that never left my side during those wet Washington winters.

It was early September, the start of fifth grade. We were in the cafeteria. Long, sticky wooden table-benches ran from wall to wall, and the pandemonium of voices made it so that I had to lean in to hear him. I hated those tables, the grime from the last lunch period, the awkward bench sitting where I had to straddle the seat for a split second and feel my weight bring the row of tables down, the way the table used to poke at my belly no matter how thin I was in fifth grade. I've felt overwhelming nausea in the cafeteria before, for several reasons. One of whom was Ryan, who happened to sit across me by the powers vested in assigned seating. I remember blushing, feeling butterflies, since he was holding my hand for some reason, and then smiling widely. At this exact moment, Ryan knew I really liked him. Like, really,

really liked it, my hand in his, his smile. I told him he was cute, while he told me I looked like an eggplant when my hair was frizzy from the rain.

How could someone I had poured so much adoration into, be so buffoonish and dense and… *mean*? So *unflinchingly* mean. He never laughed with me, just *at* me, and with the cruel recognition that his words meant so much to me. That was the beginning of the end. The extinction of my nervous butterflies, and heart flutters, and blushing. Instead, in so many ways, I molded myself into Ryan: became stand-offish, almost cool-minded, withholding any emotions or reactions, and holding my mother's hand in public. I felt as though the more I was like him, the more he'd like me back, if he'd even consider liking me back. In retrospect, I never had a chance.

Oh, the sincerity of a first love. A first infatuation and longing. I didn't even want him in any other way but pure. I just wanted to hang out with him at recess and laugh at his jokes. Hold his hand, turn magenta, and write about him in my diary. I wanted to let him take my breath away with every shy glance and smile in my direction. I didn't even want to meet his friends; I would have been more than happy with a secret between us. Like that convoluted alien invasion that he had envisioned for our school in a dream. Or the way he would keep looking at Chloe (eventually, I realized his eyes were on Kendall). I wanted to be his friend, and I would have happily accepted what was within my reach.

He made me feel ugly, unworthy of his attention, fat, the other. He made me conscious of the spices I smelled like, the *haldi, garam masala*, and *heeng*. He made me doubt my size and shape and my identities, my Indian-ness. He was the reason behind the tasteless potato-bread, cream cheese sandwiches at lunch and the nausea I'd feel after making eye contact with him. He made me conscious of everything I embodied, and so I started to doubt my own body. I doubted my intelligence, and my reading level, and my intellect. I was ten. Then I started to manifest that doubt into insecurity. Obviously, he didn't know the extent to which I liked him and his presence, but he knew enough. He knew I cared, and I would listen to him, and I would indulge his stupid boyish fantasies of alien invasions and funny Xbox usernames.

I shouldn't blame Ryan. He didn't have the mental capacity at the age of ten to fall in love with me. He didn't have the foresight or the precognition to notice just *how* much I would have done for him. My first love was too strong for our age, an age before stress and real homework, before teenage hormones and expedited adolescence. Before sex ever had a place in love. So, while I kept falling and flailing more hopelessly in love with him, we grew up and he went away.

I grew up too soon and never got to see him again. Hence, I wallowed in my own unrequited love and spilled my guts only to Rumi… too many years later. So many years later that the next time I saw him was online, and on Kendall's Face-book wall, in a homecoming photo-shoot wearing a tuxedo. When that day arrived, I felt his spirit that had lingered in my body leave. My heart's walls had broken down from each hammering, each word that slipped out of my mouth, each moment I didn't see him. I didn't love him the same way, and I wouldn't ever again.

Suddenly, I was lighter, freer, maybe even happier. I was ready to fall hopelessly in love with another Ryan.

VII

TOMBOY

———

WASHINGTON, 19 FEBRUARY 2020

With a sour scent in the air and the fan whirring away loudly, she fell in love with Princess Nokia in her full glory as a tomboy. Her heart raced and her mind blanked. In some ways, she had reached an age of maturity that escaped her at fifteen. She felt like she had succeeded in what she had attempted as a young high schooler. She was successful in the sense that she was content. Contentment motivated many of her actions that night with *him*. She sought the company of a kind stranger across the country and satisfied her physical needs. Then, mentally, she balanced the web of white lies she told herself and her folks with the erratic pounding in her brain. Words sat on the tip of her tongue, swishing around with saliva and back into her belly. She couldn't form anything so clean and pure as she had last time. No, this was dirtier. Less chaste. An urgency washed over her and she sighed at the time: 5 a.m. She only had a few hours before her alarm went off in the morning.

Time was what was running out. She'd never felt the strain of the minutes as much as she had living in Washington. An inescapable strain that forced her to the realization that she wanted to leave. She remembered the things she had wanted from her college life, and the things she had never received during those twelve months. *A good fuck for one*, she thought snarkily. Instead she spent the nights in her parents' house, lusting after men and climaxing on her childhood bedspread. *I might as well have fun*, she justified. Of course, she was terrified of ever meeting one of her online compatriots at the local Whole Foods or meeting them secretly for an afternoon tryst. So she cocooned herself in her bedroom and listened to the noises of the fan and her playlist mixing. A wall of impenetrable sound that she hoped masked any other deeds she was doing at the crack of dawn.

"Fuck." Nat swore under her breath, forcing her eyelids open, and feeling the warmth leaving the room. The sun was a dull yellow from outside, barely entering the space. Nevertheless, a sticky layer of sweat coated her chest as she sat up groggily and checked her phone. It was 9 a.m. Too early to be awake after a night of pseudo-debauchery. She squinted at her phone again, reflexively, noting the severe drought of notifications. Nat snorted and pulled the covers back up to her neck. Yet, even under her comforter and another blanket, she remained just as cold. Her hands were freezing as were her feet.

Feet.

This was all because of her feet—or, she interjected, any feet really. She had distanced herself so well from *him*. But, in a bout to prove herself worthy of his attention, or maybe to prove to herself that she could get attention, she had done a lot more than feet. She'd felt accomplished in any case. Basking in the sounds of *his* purported favorite song—a bit bland, maybe, reminding her of her own 80s kick—she waited for *his* response. *He* went to school, so while she waited impatiently, she knew not to really expect anything until tonight.

Tonight.

Last night would be tough to recreate. The black tank-top hid her belly and accentuated everything else. She looked good in some angles, looked worse in others. Would *he* care she was fat, so long as she offered him a fuck? *He* probably would, subconsciously. No one wants the fat one. She knew this too. It was eating at her. As soon as she had woken up, her eyes had passed the app icon several times, longing for a buzz or a popup. She'd gotten a singular notification and replied half an hour later, almost conspicuously on the dot. So, she busied herself in the last *Millennium* trilogy book. Barely focusing on the words, she ignored Lisbeth's miraculous recovery and instead listened to the words of Frank Ocean's "White Ferrari." She almost wanted to promise *him* a forever deal. She stopped herself short and looked sheepishly towards the empty bed next to her.

It wasn't like *he* was even here. She didn't even know if *he* was real. Nat did know, though, that when *he'd* hit her up later in the day she'd respond quickly and with ease. She wanted to interact and to connect and to fuck.

Fuck.

This was all that motivated these conversations, right? Lust and the false agency one forms at adulthood. She profoundly understood her dependency on her parents yet sought acting out in small, relatively harmless ways. Relatively because she would never be able to control anyone's actions. She wouldn't be able to control *him* if *he* leaked those fully clothed, suggestive images. Or her words. Oh, her words would be the death of her one day. Listening to *his* favorite song, she reworked her opinion. It wasn't bland, just too pure for her to feel anymore. She'd felt the exact emotions of falling in love again but never really. It was a pseudo-emotion, a placebo that her heart and mind had created in tandem so as to challenge her. Then she decided to tell *him* the truth about her weight and her… body? That was it, right? Her weight? Everything else was normal human behavior and characteristics. She didn't have the prettiest face, she knew, but would that stop anyone if she showed real interest? Real lust?

One big red flag was recognizing *his* toxic behaviors in questionably worded verses. She'd associated guys with song lyrics before, but she'd known those guys for a lot longer than *him*. Hence, this troubled her greatly. Her mouth felt drier than before and her feet were still cold. It had been so long she'd forgotten what falling in love was. Uh oh.

Now, she was listening to music with hard beats and soft voices. They reflected her personality now, a dichotomy of sorts. She wanted to hear pain in her singers' voices while being lulled into a quiet sleep. Frank Ocean's *Blond* was naturally one of the best choices. She realized she'd have to grow up sooner or later. Drive on California roads, wear low-cut tops, flirt with her eyes, and shop responsibly for groceries. All the signs of a real woman.

This time, her playlist was really singing to her. Every song felt relevant, helpful even. And she imagined herself dancing slowly alone in a club. Or at least what she perceived a club to be as she had never been to one before. Something like in *Saturday Night Fever,* with a disco ball and a dance floor and coordinated choreography. Her hips swinging, her hair flying, eyes closed. Hopefully, her overall appearance would dissuade any boy from approaching her. *It had before*, she grimaced sourly. *But boys were boys and men are men*, she supposed. There is an invalidated difference, even if she herself hadn't experienced it. She remembered the men or old men who ghosted her after seeing her face. That was it. One picture and they were suddenly better than her. There was no talk about how her age should have been enough to stop them.

Nat thought about the ring on her finger. It sat comfortably in its position, her left ring finger. She wasn't engaged, and she never wanted to convey that, but she liked it there. It made her feel engaged to herself in a way. She had to focus on herself before focusing on anyone else irl—in real life—as though her online life was all a lie. But to her, it felt more real than life did sometimes because it was tangible. There was an immediate response. Men begged and reacted appropriately or as she wanted them to. Every glimpse in the mirror or black mirror in her hands reminded her otherwise though. In real life, she'd probably never experienced these emotions so truly. Everyone was horny online, and their goal was simple: find a girl/guy/person willing to subdue their horniness. It's not a new concept, just that the dance has changed quite a bit in the last twenty years. Natasha would know, she'd been at it for more than five.

Had she made a mistake in trusting *him*? A complete stranger? She didn't even know which school *he* went to, if *he* did at all. Okay, she gave *him* a little more credit than that. *He* felt sincere, real in a way. Flawed and a bit manipulative, sure. But she played into *his* manipulations willingly. She knew what she was doing. She'd been an adult living alone up until a month ago. Seriously, in November she was shopping for groceries and going to school full-time. *That had to count for something, right…?*

He *hasn't called me a slut*, she pinched herself. *That's new.* That's a new thing she'd noticed this time around. Men were kinder to her for some reason, a little more forgiving and seductive. They didn't want her to run. Maybe it was #MeToo coming full circle, or she was talking to those enlightened individuals the news doesn't mention. Or they liked the fact she was nineteen and virginal.

Was I too harsh on him? *I barely know* him *or his* life. *Honestly, he was probably just busy, and I shouldn't have laid it on* him *like that. Though I just asked if* he *regretted what we did last night and felt embarrassed. I deserve to know! Or chances are,* he's *just busy. Or chances are also,* he's *seething and I'm about to find my ass on... what are the leak sites again? Isn't it almost 6 p.m.? Maybe* he *had a full day of classes. Why do I care?*

Why do I care?

Maybe it was because February was scurrying away, and she didn't have anything to show for it but a few lost pounds. And, her rest. And, the fact that she hadn't had a severe acne breakout in the last two months. Her peace of mind, she's recovering. *It's almost like rehab*, she justified again. *If rehab allowed microdosing.* The thing she needed to extricate herself from—her phone—was still in her hands, her fingers in a dizzying scroll. Maybe she wasn't as satisfied with scrolling through TikToks right now, but for how long would this homemade solution work?

So, as usual she ignored her problems and watched a man detail a car boot for twenty minutes.

Forcing herself out of her bed, she ran her fingers through her hair and tied a ponytail. Nat started daydreaming about *him* again in the weirdest of ways as she scrubbed her skin and let the showerhead smack some sense, in the form of pelting droplets of water, into her. Hastily drying herself off, she went into her closet and eyed her choices.

Today was a boy day.

She just felt like emulating one. Instead of the body-hugging tank-top from last night, she chose a baggy shirt and her favorite grey shorts. She thought they made her ass look nice which was reason enough to keep them around. She purposely hadn't responded to *him* yet, though she did feel bad about it. She wanted to see what *he* said, how *he* said it, if *he* meant it, and if not, what they'd do about it. *Was* he *going to meticulously try to turn her on again, like* he *had been doing for several days now? Was it over in so few words or less?*

Bathed and clothed, she contemplated as she walked the thirty steps to the living room couch and television. Waiting for the TV's electronic hum to begin, she started clicking through the catalog of free movies. Her phone was still in her pocket, untouched; she could almost feel the ghost of a vibration.

The sun had barely set and she was already in front of the television, cross-legged on the sticky couch. The dark room created a false sense of time, making it feel a lot later than it was. Her breath caught as she imagined *him* next to her, an arm around her waist or somewhere more exciting. Shaking her head, Nat snapped herself out of it with a slight shiver. She needed to find a movie, something preferably free and mindless. At least, one of the good old things would take her mind off *him*, right? *Primal Fear* it is. *Fitting*, she thought macabrely, *but so not sexy. Even better!* The film started and her mind wandered as the title sequence rolled.

She had overthought it. *He* was busy, and she had acted like an ass. *Fitting.* She turned her notifications on again and just waited, feeling as though a weight had lifted off of her shoulders. She still felt like an ass, only this time she actually felt it as compared to those quick moments that stung but never stuck around for the entire day...

Why am I awake at 2:44 a.m. on a Wednesday night? Why and who on Earth am I doing this for? Is this completely selfish and stupid? Or am I worried for some reason? I'm anxious, that's true. I have some mild insomnia to battle. I haven't spoken to my therapist in two weeks and I'm breaking down more and more every moment. This sucks. I just want a warm body next to me - one I didn't exit out of on the fateful day of my birth. Someone who I could feel behind me. Someone that actually existed within a ten-mile radius who responded to my bombardment of messages. And who reciprocated whatever stupid feelings I had caught accidentally. I wasn't supposed to. This was supposed to be chill and it started that way before I fucking went ahead and fucked it up. I'm suspended in a conversation, waiting for a response that'll take more than just a few hours. And the tumult grows and expands until it distorts my perspective.

Swallowing, Nat realized it was half-past three in the morning, and she had been waiting for nearly the entire night for *his* reply. Her mum had somehow entered the room without her realizing and switched on a completely differ-ent movie.

So much for distractions.

VIII

WHOLE FOODS

——

This was a meeting she had imagined for a very long time.

She'd be browsing the pasta aisle—her favorite in the store—looking at the overpriced dried noodles directly imported from Italy. She'd bend down and accidentally brush up against someone. Not just anyone, someone with strong arms, curly black hair, and a nice smile, who'd laugh it off and offer to grab something for her from the top shelf. She sees it in slow-motion. The sunlight filtering through the windows, and past them, hitting her hair so beautifully. She'd laugh with him and ask for something, gesturing that she couldn't quite get past a certain height; she'd stand on her tiptoes, and hope his eyes would fall to her lips then her chest as she got back down to the ground. A little wandering didn't hurt anybody. She would raise her brows slightly when noticing the fancy University of Virginia sweatshirt, and lanyard hanging out of his pocket.

(This is where in Nat's fantasy, the realities of sexual harassment would take over for her; she didn't want a man to objectify her body, but she had never seen it in action and was curious to see how it would make her feel. She'd interject that, while public gawking and whistling was horrendous

for most women, she'd never been on either side of that coin. Hence, her fantasy was based on the countless media images of a meet-cute and not any real interactions with men.)

She'd smile again, this time more shyly, and… turn back around to the dried Italian noodles.

(Even in her fantasies, she couldn't imagine a guy asking her out or doing more than helping or just existing in the same space.)

From noodles, her hands would travel to pasta sauces as she'd pick each one up and scan the lengthy ingredient list, feeling her eyes glaze over with boredom and annoyance. Maybe he'd clear his throat and recommend one; on the off chance it didn't have meat, she'd swoon slightly before asking if he were a vegetarian. He would respond in the affirmative, and joke about never being able to get good cheese.

"I actually just became vegan, so that's been different."

"To be honest, I'm kind of a bad vegetarian," she'd chuckle, and feel a sharp desire in her belly. "I still buy aged Parm. I can't get enough of it, ya know?!" She'd end sheepishly, and flush slightly as his piercing eyes raked over her again.

(This is when she'd pause again and debate the motions of this, honestly, quite awkward interaction. Now, vegetarianism was a covertly casteist practice that she could not seem to get rid of. Mainly because she figured if she were already this fat without meat, steak would really kill her poor heart. No matter how incredible Gordon Ramsey's beef wellington looked.)

"Here, have you tried this sauce?"

He'd reach for a jar above her head, and she'd catch a whiff of his cologne. Biting her lip, she'd accept it from him and put it into her cart. She was willing to commit to the pasta sauce. Was he willing to commit to at least one date?

Hesitantly, she'd ask him, "Have any good date-night recipes?"

And, he'd respond, "Yeah. Though I do have some better ideas than just pasta."

Then, they'd dance out of the store in true Indian movie style before riding off into the sunset.

(Curly Black Hair (CBH) was not her soulmate, she already knew that. No, he was just someone who'd make her feel better after having her heart broken so many times. They'd enjoy the time spent together, make love furiously, fall in fatuation, and go their separate ways like adults. CBH was a mystery, an unachievable entity. Everyone wanted love, if they knew it or not, in some way. CBH was the perfect complement to her kind of love, which is what she sought. Or, to put it more delicately, it was the mutual understanding that sealed their love. Temporary, transient romance. Canned romance, almost, perfectly acceptable to put on display in front of a studio audience on the set of a sitcom. Like canned tomatoes were perfectly acceptable to use in *MasterChef*, so long as they were from San Marzano. Nat wondered where the San Marzano of love was.)

IX

WHAT IF?

I wonder if Ryan is my ideal man. Or at least, the curly, black-haired one that'll sweep me off my feet. Too bad he has flat blonde hair without any volume or body. Too bad he wouldn't have asked me if I preferred alfredo over marinara. Too bad Ryan is still probably a jerk.

But what if I met Ryan today? Bumped into him at Whole Foods, or Chipotle. Saw him with clear eyes and refocused my feelings onto myself. What if I didn't laugh as much at his jokes or steal glances at him surreptitiously? What if I found myself hating his appearance or his presence? What if, when I met him, he recognized me accurately as the girl who liked him first? What if he joked about my crush, my puppy love, my unrequited intensity? Would I be angry? Would I be pissed off at his nonchalance as I had been so many years ago? Would I feel bitter?

Fuck that. But why the fuck not?

Bitterness would fuel my other actions and reactions. A smirk and not a smile. A mumbled, under-my-breath comment and lackluster response. Would my heart still stop at the sight of him? Did he still unknowingly have that power over me? Would I be emboldened by my newfound sensuality? My now nineteen-year-old body? A vessel that would only last another few months.

A newly emerged twenty-year-old would enter the world. My age wouldn't change a lot about my inherent personality. I would just feel the passing of time crawling through my veins and blood cells. Forcing my body to stop regenerating faster than it started dying. I would age, physically, the lines on my face and skin wouldn't just disappear. My expressions would freeze. What if I were more angry than happy? What if the indent between my eyebrows deepened every time I scowled? What if every throaty chuckle stayed in place, enhancing my crow's-feet and laugh lines? What if my acne scars never left? What if my hairline further receded and I was forced to reckon with oddly requisitioned male-pattern balding?

Would I still seek Ryan's appreciation? A pleasant appraisal of my physicality rather than my layered life full of emotions, experience, and intelligence? My uncanny ability to… remember, and problem solve, and listen, carefully, empathetically. Would that be accompanied by the confidence I feel in a classroom?

What if I received his appreciation? A stray compliment, or an unnecessary smile, or glance in my direction? What if he never noticed me? What if I blended into the crowd in the food court, my cute pants and body-hugging shirt going over his head? What if my confidence didn't matter to him? What if he liked my insecurity more than he did me? Why did I even have to be insecure, to perform for him?

What if I saw Ryan and he didn't mean anything to me? What if my heart didn't stop and my breath didn't catch midair? What if I recognized him, and felt nothing leave my body? What if my soul didn't lighten its weight? What if he flags me down? Would I care then? What if he matched with me on Tinder? Am I supposed to wait until he messages first? Could I ask him out? Could we finally give it—what I had been longing for—a shot? Would he even reciprocate my interest? Would he even be interesting? What if I bared my soul to him, like I had done in the past, and what if Ryan actually became a reality?

What if I didn't want Ryan at all? What if what I actually want is to recreate the same, hardened hatred I felt for myself so many years ago but in another person? What if I wanted someone to hurt as much as I had? What if I'm not a good person?

Would that be so bad?

PART II

LOVE AT
FIRST SEXT

XI

ARUNDHATI-VASISHTHA

—

WASHINGTON, 14 APRIL 2020

Nat adored her parents. An outsider might think she was a bit bitter about how her genetics turned out, or how she was spoiled rotten growing up, or how she never had to face any true adversity even after moving continents and cities and houses and schools. Yet, she wasn't. She couldn't be, not after all that they had done and continued to do for her. Nat loved her parents, and many times realized she was living for them. They guided the most meaningful decisions in her life, and she had withered away without them in college. Her parents ardently believed in her and her abilities; she didn't even believe in herself half as much sometimes.

Growing up, she never fully comprehended her parents' relationship. They looked, spoke, behaved, and complemented each other like two really close roommates. She never saw them as lovers, which was maybe a result of her upbringing and naivety with love. Maybe that whole roommates thing didn't really have legs. Nevertheless, she loved them wholeheartedly. She loved their conversations, their silly quarrels, their nicknames for each other ("Gigi" for her mum, and "Adi" for her dad, whose full name was a heavy Vikramaditya), their twin smiles, her mum's side eye and her dad's constant urge to fidget…

A younger Vikram was disciplined, a bit too well-versed in his future, ambitious with a *keeda* or parasite that forced him to keep on keeping on. He walked around with a half-scowl, clenched teeth, and his shoulders near his ears, wound up and stressed. Vikram grew up as the first-born son, weighed down by the requirements of his parents and expectations of himself. An angry young man.

An older Vikram, the man she knew better as her dad, was less of a disciplinarian than one might imagine. He was their family's catalyst, the first one to join a big American university for his master's degree and essentially improved all their futures: hers, her mum's, and even, their extended clan. Her dad was talkative and boisterous—someone Nat instantly recognized as a potential frat boy, if given the opportunity. But his underlying seriousness hadn't left him altogether. He was prone to long silent spells after a bad day at work, in front of the television, while Nat and her mum argued about something petty. Then, he would break his silence with a long, painful whine for his own mother—Nat's *Ajji*—and launch into a conversation about said day at work.

Nat remembered the first time she learnt about the stock market when she was nine, using Colgate as an example, and guided by her father Vikram. Distribution of shares, market capitalization, stock prices, Wall Street. Her father was far from businesslike, though. No matter what, at the end of the day, he always had time to spend with his family. They visited parks, walked for hours, and drove to scenic view-points. They listened to music blasting in the car and rode their bikes to the waterfront. He took care of his family first, no matter what.

Her mother, Geet, was a U-turn in another direction, as all U-turns are. Her mum's family was a lot more chill, almost zany in a way. They moved from city to city as an army family and were posted all over India. Geet developed an uncanny ability to distance herself from stress as well as react too strongly. She was cool, collected, and philosophical. Geet didn't live in the past or the future, instead with her head on her shoulders, eyes on the ground, focusing on each step, each moment. Geet lived in the present, in the moment. Even as the eldest of three, Geet was the natural peacemaker. When she did eventually explode, it would always be pur-poseful and built up over several weeks. And generally, directed at the walls rather than her family. Though, she rarely shouted at her daughter.

In fact, her mum never truly got angry unless Nat had said something particularly hurtful—which she had in the past, as a younger, angstier teenager. Nat was just looking for a reaction most of those times and had cruelly baited her mother into feeling those emotions. Geet was practical, and extraor-dinarily irrational at the same frustrating time. Nat and her mum never seemed to agree on a lot of things but miraculously they remained close confidantes. Nat knew intrinsically she was a lot like her mum, but also too much like her dad to ever see eye-to-eye with Geet. Nat was still angry, and still young; she just hoped one day, she would mellow down, too. Her mum also had a tendency to smooth over their disagreements as agreements. Geet was the first person to tell Nat to confess her attraction to a few poor boys in her first-grade class.

"It's useless to hide those kinds of things!" Geet had said while helping a six-year-old Nat button up her dress.

Eventually, that advice bit her in the rear when the boy she had liked didn't like her back. As did every boy she had ever liked. After Nat came back home disappointed, Geet had brushed it off. "It's okay, *beta*. At least, you told him and now he knows!" In any case, her mum was always willing to listen, even if Nat didn't want to talk.

Her parents were an odd couple, definitely, yet oddly alike in so many random ways. *They smiled the same*, Nat always remarked to herself. She had inherited that toothy grin.

If destiny hadn't intervened, her *doctor-thatha* wouldn't have seen Geet's matrimonial ad in the newspaper. Or enquired about her family in common army circles. Vikram, then, wouldn't have requested her *Major-thatha*'s permission to phone his eldest daughter, his "pearl child." Nat's parents wouldn't have ever spoken for two hours on their first call and approved of each other.

"If it's a yes for him, it's a yes for me."

    "If it's a yes for her, it's a yes for me."

If life hadn't intervened, her parents would never have met. Vikram hadn't even seen Geet's photograph when they decided to get engaged. Nat craved that kind of delectably sweet, almost fictional romance. Meeting each other virtually, falling in love, and then committing to a lifetime together. Other than being a super *filmi* love story, it was also really wholesome. One summer, Nat had stumbled upon some of the love letters and faxes her parents had sent each other nearly two decades earlier. She almost felt embarrassed, before realizing there was nothing really provocative or awkwardly sexual in them. They were just sweet and full of puppy love. In strange ways, her parents' early relationship reminded her of *him*: long-distance, virtual, never even seen his face. *Mum and dad are a forever deal, this is just a fling,* she'd force upon herself, *not the threads of fates at play.* Right? It was a bad habit, nonetheless.

If that love hadn't intervened, Vikram would have stayed in the US and Geet in India. Instead, her parents rushed between both countries trying to reconcile with each other. They sent each other their hand-written letters and spoke on the phone for hours. Her mum stayed up writing about her own restlessness, her love for this near stranger. It was a whirlwind six months that ended in marriage and a New Years' Eve in New York City.

At times, in their wedding pictures, they looked like models stuck in motion and suppressing their excitement to be wed. Their wedding photographers had spared no expense, or time, in taking pictures of the bride, the groom, the sisters, and the brothers. Nat had pored over their wedding album a dozen times, trying to recognize her parents in the fresh-faced twenty-somethings that posed with wide grins and in high spirits. This time, looking over the photos again, Nat became curious with the heavy album under her nose.

"Mama, where did you get married?" She was sitting at the kitchen's island, flanked by her mum making tea on the stove.

"Hm, *beta*?" Her mum was looking at her phone, distracted. Geet turned to her daughter, still stirring the milky *chai*. The scent of cardamom, *elaichi*, and ginger wafted towards Nat.

"Where did you get married?"

"Bangalore, where else?" Geet shrugged, and rolled her eyes at Nat. Her mum was still in her pyjamas, even though it was way past noon.

"No, I mean, like, where *in* the city did you get married?"

"Oh. Well, the building doesn't exist anymore, but it was a big hall near where your *Major-thatha* and *Ammama* live."

"Oh, interesting…" Nat paused, noticing a picture of her *Major-thatha* and her dad. "Wait, mama, what are they doing here?" Squinting, Nat leaned in closer to see her *Major-thatha* holding an umbrella over her dad's head and offering her dad a banana. Her dad was grinning from ear to ear, almost sheepishly. In the next photo, her dad was taking a sip from a steel glass.

"One sec, *beta*." Geet poured the tea from the saucepan into the line of six cups on the counter, carefully removing and replacing the strainer on top of each vessel. Geet peered over Nat's shoulder. "Let me see?" Pulling the album towards her, Geet furrowed her brow before breaking into a chuckle. "Oh! These photos."

Geet explained how *Major-thatha* was supposed to mash the banana and mix it with the warm milk before feeding the concoction to Vikram. "Daddy was always very smart. Instead of being messy, he just peeled the banana. See?" She pointed to the half-peeled banana, and Nat laughed.

"Wait, so, you're not supposed to do that?"

"No… But we're a weird family, *baba*. It'd take a lot more than a banana to stop that." Geet winked at her daughter and hummed as she took a long sip from her tea. "Ah… Did you want tea, *beta*?"

Nat eyed the row of cups and shrugged. "I guess. Is there Parle-G?"

"Let me check!"

"Wait, actually, can you just tell me what you're doing here?"

"In South Indian Hindu weddings," Geet explained matter-of-factly. "The couple tries—many times in the middle of the day like your dad and I—to find the Great Bear, or Ursa Major, constellation." Another long sip of tea, and she continued. "Or as it's known in Indian astronomy, *Saptarishi* or Seven Great Sages. Within the constellation are two stars that orbit each other, attracted to each other's gravity."[1]

"Hm, wow. So, like, these old ancient scientists knew how to find these stars with the naked eye?" Nat remarked.

"Yeah," Geet sat down next to her at the island and pulled the laptop towards her. She started looking up the details. "I think they're called Arundhati and Vasishtha." Geet pushed the screen towards Nat and returned to nursing her piping hot *chai*.

The symbolism wasn't lost on Nat. Forcing young couples to emulate the behavior of inanimate objects light-years away was the most pedantically Hindu thing ever. But, the idea is that in a relationship there needs to be equality; as one does, so does the other. Give and take. An equitable understanding. A dual orbit, caused by attraction to each other rather than in service of one. Division of labor, of love, of life. Trust. Friendship. Open communication. Effortless maintenance. The space for forgiveness and consequences, as deemed appropriately. All qualities of a healthy relationship.

Nat never really saw that between her parents; it always felt as though one parent was giving more or doing more. To her, it was inherently unequal, but it wasn't her place to judge as their child. Nevertheless, Nat didn't *get* how they knew concretely they were right for each other without ever having known each other beyond a telephone-fax connection. Neither of her parents had ever dated before or even attempted romantic relationships. But, at twenty-nine and twenty-eight they made the life-altering decision to get married to each other. That they were each other's "Person," the One.

---

1 M.K.V. Narayan, *Flipside of Hindu Symbolism: Sociological and Scientific Linkages in Hinduism* (Fultus Books, 2007), 150.

She reflected on the past two months. The whirlwind of the first three weeks. Meeting *him* on Valentine's Day.

Tasting his name on her lips for the first time: *Ben*.

Speaking to each other just enough to keep the other person intrigued. Losing some of her firsts with him. If this were a movie, Ben would be her endgame. Stupidly so, maybe, definitely. The guy she ends up with, but in this case, out of necessity and naivety. Neither of them had been with another person before. They were probably just tantalized by the *prospect* of each other, not an actual reality. Ben wasn't her One. But, again, who says there only needs to be one?

XII

ASL

——

4:36 PM, 2/21/2020

brattypatty is online
tanning.chatum is online

brattypatty is typing...

is it....
Brock
Brandon
Beowolf

Lmao wtf no
Okkkkkk
I'll give you a hint
Its short
Like yours ;)

Uhhh... idfk
Ben lmao

Bran like GoT
Bryan

O.O

What lol?

You got it

Bryan???

Noooo
Its Ben

Oh
Well, it's nice to meet you, Ben! ;D

Nice to meet you too Nat

Wait, do you go to like college?

Yeah haha

Lmao, what year in school are ya?
Major?

Sophomore
Im in business

Huh, nice. Me too!
Lol, how old are you? :3

Im 19

o;
me too

Lol nice
Wbu

I'm doing Bio rn
Probs thinking of med school
But like not sure yet haha
Which school do you go to, if you don't mind my asking?

Wow
You must b hella smart
Well rn I go to community college but Im finna get into uva

Oh neat.
I have a couple friends there lol
Not really

Wait
Can you help me with some hw then

Lol what?
What kinda hw

Uh
Intro to Bio
its supposed to be teh easiest section

Um, lol, ok???

XIII

CITY OF STARS

———

Living with the stars, like a star of her own. Never in her life had Nat felt like she was anything less than an angel to her parents. Adorned and adored, loved and cared for, pampered and scrubbed. Every day of her life until she couldn't take it anymore. She remembered the first time visiting LA as a young child, living near the beach for a few days, eating fast food, and going to Disneyland. Huntington Beach, if she recalled correctly. Then, her second visit a decade later. She hated it, abhorred it really. The dirt and grime stood out to her, more than anything, the kitschy lights and obnoxiously American Hollywood sign. Repulsed at the filth and the dreariness of the people. *LA was where dreams died*, she had thought. *No one was really happy or satisfied in LA, just trying to go through the motions of life.*

After the trip, she began to fantasize about New York. The glitz and glam. Fashion Week. Late night television. She remembered navigating the skyscrapers of Manhattan, the views of the Brooklyn Bridge from Dumbo, the Wall Street Bull, Central Park, Rockefeller Plaza on her four-inch touchscreen. All places and names she'd picked up from *New York Nights,* the iPod game, more than a decade earlier. Curious how JFK seemed so familiar even when she had never even been to LaGuardia. Enthralled by the promise of building a life, creating her own dream rather than reaching for one marketed to her, living in the fast lane, drawn to the ruthless ambition and backstabbing she presumed existed in all walks of East Coast living.

Instead, she learnt to pause in college, even after years of dreaming about New York. Passing by the olive trees, feeling the slick ground as she crushed leftover olives, watching the sun peek through the branches and prompt her to wear her sunglasses. In college, she had forgotten those ambitions, or backstabbing, had a place in the real world. Instead, she preferred to listen to people walking by her dorm window, the wind rustling on leaves, and feel the cool air on her skin after nightfall. She waited for those precious moments every day, time to herself and her room.

As the Malibu wildfires raged, her first semester poofed by like a cloud of gray, noxious gas. She breathed in the dust and pollution that cast a hazy glow over her campus, squinting her eyes behind her glasses, and feeling them burn slightly. The smoke remained a constant companion for nearly three months. LA became her refuge. Closer to the flames, yes, but far enough to share the smoke with strangers surrounding her. She enjoyed the late-night strolls, the noise, the cars zooming by every once in a while. Maybe a B-List celeb or an influencer spending that endorsement money. She enjoyed the idea of LA. Maybe enough to start loving it. Enough to miss it over the breaks, and the weekends.

She reminisced about the twenty-minute walk from Union Station to Little Tokyo. Dodging past eight-wheelers, a news camera (bizarre!), and through an industrial part of Downtown. Under a freeway, across the road. The sweat that had accumulated on her forehead. The red backpack whose straps dug into her shoulder, and a duffel bag she carried her clothes in. She had gotten a good workout that day, walking less than a mile, hefting at least fifteen extra pounds. Her shirt had stuck to her back and she felt conscious of sitting inside the air-conditioned ramen place with her backpack off. And, of her stench.

She'd always been ultra-conscious of her smells, good and bad. Indian families rarely care about smell. But her family made a big drama of closing every door in their house to protect their clothes and rooms from the spices wafting throughout the kitchen and up in the vents. It was a Sisyphean task. No matter what they'd do, the spices would stick to their pores and hair and in the back of their sinuses. Not bad smells, no. Delicious smells, food-smells. Stinky foods that white people weren't used to, so Nat pretended not to be used to them either. And, enjoyed her mushy, lukewarm potato-bread sandwiches. But as soon as she hit puberty, deodorant became her best friend. Her mum didn't like antiperspirants for her pubescent daughter, only the organic, non-aluminum, weak ones from Whole Foods. Nat started wearing perfume heavily and carrying deodorant every day. So, while she sat through her own body odor in classrooms, she hoped no one else could smell her. Most of the time, people can only smell themselves. The sun was not good for her smells, but here she was, living in the sunniest place in America.

When she was sixteen, Nat saw *La La Land*. Then, she saw it again. And, again. Some movies were meant to be seen more than once, because if they weren't re-watched the viewer loses the essence of the film. The juice, the bone marrow which can only be relished after picking off the meat.

Usually, in films like *La La Land,* the marrow is found in its layers, well-hidden beneath the ditsy star-cast and performances. Nat never liked it, even after the fourth viewing, surrounded by her friends in a dark orchestra room. When she did find the essence, she fell in love with the film. It was the music. So obvious, so surface-level, so basic. But, the music moved the film. The catchy opening track "Another Day of Sun," and the heart-wrenching love motif "Mia & Sebastian's Theme." She felt one with the characters so clearly that she was genuinely angry at the ending. The doomed love affair, Seb's obsession with jazz, Mia's indifference to him when he comes back for her.[2] La La Land also happened to be a nickname for Los Angeles.

Los Angeles. Suddenly, she was hopelessly in love with LA. The sun, the traffic, the stupid number of neighborhoods (without shortened nicknames, looking at you Tribeca. Why do you have "triangle" in your name?!), its sprawl from Santa Monica to Boyle Heights, the freezing desert nights. She was in love with how she felt every time she would visit; boarding the Metrolink, riding for an hour, and feeling awestruck at Union Station (*but,* she'd interject, *I haven't been to Grand Central yet*). So massive, so colossal, so imposing. While in college, she imagined a life in LA. Driving for two hours, living in some ground-floor condo, wanting to walk to the corner shop but taking her car to a fancy grocery store instead.

California. Los Angeles. "City of Stars."

The song that weighed heavily on her heart and mind. The motif was truly painful even after four viewings and deconstructing the melody. She had spent weeks re-writing

---

2   *La La Land,* directed by Damien Chazelle (2015; Los Angeles, CA: Warner Bros. Pictures, 2016).

it for a class project, and even in its simplest form, it haunted her. The feelings between Mia and Sebastian haunted her. The thought of ever abandoning a love so beautiful was a frightening, shiver-inducing tragedy. She thought of Norma Desmond's eyes in *Sunset Boulevard*, the sadness enshrined within her pupils, her loneliness, her mania. She wouldn't know how to end a relationship, end love. She tried her best to *end* it with Ryan, but what was there to end, if nothing had ever begun? With Ben, had anything even started? Had she just fallen into the same trap as she had with Ryan?

Falling in love with the idea of love with a person, without accounting for the person themselves?

Without considering Ben as a real human being on the other side of a touchscreen, young and lonely? But not desperate enough to fall in love with a fat stranger across the country. She feared she'd feel it too deeply, intensely, allow it to permeate her bones. She was scared she'd lose someone who loved every inch of her, including her sweat, and insecurities. That this someone didn't exist at all. That if they did, they might leave her. And, that once this person left, she'd never find someone again, and she'd be forced to relive Joe's last moments, face down in a pool, shot in the head.[3] Or worse… face down in a pool, shot by an ex-lover's husband à la Jay Gatsby.[4]

Or even worse… they'd be alive, well, and happy with a small, growing family, living their dream life that never included her.

But, for any of that to happen, she'd have to live in New York.

---

3   *Sunset Boulevard*, directed by Billy Wilder (1950; Los Angeles, CA: Paramount Pictures, 1950).

4   F. Scott Fitzgerald, *The Great Gatsby*. (New York: Charles Scribner's Sons, 1925).

XIV

BEN

——

VIRGINIA, 7 MARCH 2020

I haven't messaged her in a while. I mean, I was the last one to text, but I want to know what she's up to. Now is a better time than any to check up on her—

Oh, she's online?

Who's she talking to now? Isn't it the middle of the day for her? Yeah, it's like noon.

It was 3 p.m. and he was in the middle of campus. There was a quiet hum of student traffic and loud music distantly playing in the background. His phone was nearly pitch-black under the sun's bright glare. Ben moved under a canopy and waited until his eyes readjusted.

He scrolled up, his eyes glancing over the few risqué pictures she had sent last night. He perked up just a little bit and cleared his throat. Looking around to make sure he was somewhat alone, he increased the brightness to high. And, bam.

There she was. Legs slightly spread. Shaved, like he had asked her. It was a short ten-second clip of something way more than he had expected. A cute titty-bounce. Ben smirked sheepishly and scrolled further up to their first conversation on **The Chatroom**. They had been talking about some random video he'd sent, a really hot one, anyway. Because it was only after he sent her at least fifteen links that she shared that *one* video.

His phone pinged, and the small green arrow showed that a message had just arrived. From her. Nat.

3:08 PM, 3/7/2020

brattypatty is online
brattypatty is typing...
hey :)

Underneath the innocuous text was a massive full-color image of her in just her underwear. She was standing sideways, with her ass almost facing the mirror, and a finger was toying with the top of her thong. *Fuck.* Ben looked around anxiously, accidentally making eye-contact with some random kid. Feeling his cheeks flush, he swore under his breath. His fingers were slightly unsteady as he decreased the brightness again. *Holy. Fuck.*

what do you think? ^.^
i literally JUST got this thong

Ben swallowed and replied shakily. He was more nervous about being caught with spontaneous amateur porn on his phone than his actual reaction to her. Fidgeting with the small scar on his jaw, he formulated a response.

Fuck babe
Im literalyy in public
You look really good
Like
If I was there rn

He could almost hear her roll her eyes and chuckle. Ben imagined that she'd have a sexy laugh, one that at least rivaled how
sexy she felt. *She was fucking confident; I'll give her props.*

haha whaaaaat???
i just came back from my workout
uggghh
B, i'm like so horny rn
it's so early too, like i can't just
you know.

Ben did know. They had done some pretty freaky things
last night. *But, fuck, if she ever did what that bitch Cassie—*
his thoughts were interrupted again by a slight vibration
and ping.

Another image of Nat in her full glory. This time, she
was completely facing the mirror and he could see her lips.
Between them, her thong.

Fuck. I gotta get back to my room, Ben thought as he
uncomfortably shifted his pants. *But, wait, don't I have class
in like fifteen?*

Baby.
LIsten
Tonite
I am gonna fuck the shit out of you

But rn I gtg
Later tonight
I swear
Your so fucking hot

Clicking his phone off, Ben stuffed it back into his backpack, vaguely feeling it vibrate through the layers of fabric. *It's probably nothing though.*

XV

"FRIENDS DON'T TREAT EACH OTHER LIKE SHIT."

—————

WASHINGTON, 25 MARCH 2020

Nat had been holding on. Holding onto something she never knew she actually had. A romance, a relationship, a friend, a best friend. She was destroyed by the idea it didn't exist in her realm as a reality. She felt isolated and lonely. She isolated and distanced. Part her fault, part the ignorance of others. *One* other. She cried every three weeks to the fastest songs in her playlist, reminding herself life was not just about the bad. Even if it felt like that. It really wasn't the case. There were always the yellow polka-dotted bits of happiness and pleasure in a sea of brown. And the hem of false hope, the silver-lining so to speak. No life was complete without a little bit of yearning.

She was jealous. Of what, she had no clue. Of whom, nobody she could think of! Okay, she could. Nat didn't want to confront the strain she had felt between herself and Rumi. How could a best friend of nearly a decade, a sister, just cease to care so much? Distance, they say, makes the heart grow fonder, but in the case of Nat and Rumi it felt as though the distance tore their relationship to bits.

All Nat could see were fragments of their memories together. Friends are even more important than lovers, Nat had noted one night after fighting the delicious urge to text Rumi. It had been nearly three weeks since their last video call. Since then Nat had essentially cultivated an entire relationship with a boy, all the way on the East Coast. So fucking far away. Who could guarantee that distance, the same kind of distance, would not just end everything? Even if it did start something so beautiful and raw between her and Ben. That's unfair. Her relationship with Ben wasn't beautiful. It was just raw.

Her phone pinged, and she was forced to reckon with the one who *did* seem to care: Ben.

9:52 PM, 3/25/2020

brattypatty is online
tanning.chatum is online

tanning.chatum is typing…
duuude
That video was hooott 

brattypatty is typing…
Ikr?!!!
I love her omg she's so fucking sexy
Like wtf it's unfair lmao

Bruhh you're pretty cute tho

like your ass is
🔥 🔥 🔥

Jeez thanks lol
I think I need to workout a lot before tho

Hmm yeah
You'll look a lot better but like
Your already pretty hot

Haha, yeah.
I just don't want my boobs to get smaller lmao

I mean
It could happen but
Itd just be some loose skin yk
So like you'd still be hot lol

Ha, thanks 🙃
Anyway, I can't believe she's younger than us!!!!

The girl in the vid
Fuuuucck
No way

I KNOW!!!!

Being deep and introspective isn't sexy, but it was who she was ninety percent of the time. Or at least, when she was being deep and introspective no one ever considered her as sexy. With Ben, she didn't even have the chance to be deep or thoughtful; she dumbed herself down for him. She knew she was insightful and observant, but she didn't want him to know. Even after several years, Nat wouldn't want men to know the breadth of her intelligence. *They'd screw with you more if they knew they could use creative ways*, she thought snarkily. She was too smart to let that happen before she fully opened herself up to someone.

She was jealous that some parts of her body were nicer than others and that those parts were the only ones Ben cared about. Sending disembodied pieces of herself wasn't going to help anyone see her more clearly or help herself be honest with him and herself. It wasn't validation when she was censoring. It was deception. She was a fat girl. She could barely see her vulva. She couldn't see her feet. What was the point of hiding that from him other than vanity? Wasn't her personality and her good parts enough? Wasn't the idea of pretty decent… subjective?

Even the kinder guys didn't acknowledge her tears. At this point, finding love was a fool's errand. *I can't live online,* she thought frantically. That meant going out into the real world, one where people didn't send notifications or react to what you say with a thumbs-up and hearts. A world where even her closest confidantes didn't really listen, and she felt herself suffocating in her forced penance. She was not silent by choice. She had ideas, too, of why she was the way she was. Maybe, she should give up personal relationships and focus on the one with her therapist. Or a relationship where imaginary hands wrapped around her massive waist and stoked the butterflies in her stomach. A relationship that felt like the shocking descent of a rollercoaster, a sharp jabbing sensation that started at her bellybutton and ended in her panties. The navel pull that reached all the way down to her knees, making her feel weaker than usual, with the same tenacity as her methods of avoiding the butterflies. Her firewalls and her VPN. Her multitude of Ryans.

She hadn't felt butterflies in years. Not on stage. Not while speaking Spanish in Peru. She didn't feel them while addressing her classmates at graduation, or when caught laughing loudly in the middle of class. Just when imagining made up scenarios and dreaming about people she'd never meet. But then they flew away again. Blubbery and false modesty and compliments never impressed her, and it had just been too long since her first love. She was over them, the butterflies.

Almost completely.

A vibration accompanied by a banner *totally* didn't make her breath shorten and her heart pound; it *definitely* didn't cause that darned navel pull. Her bravado had slipped one night, and her vulnerability was apparent. It was her body. It had always been, but he had been too thick to notice in the first few days.

Or maybe Ben ignored her body to see where their words took them. She was the one who offered a picture first. Then, another. And another. Then she acquiesced to his preferences, without any urging from him. She just wanted to, for him. A small gift to thank him for all the positive feelings he had brought into her life. Misplaced appreciation, she realized, as Ben never knew what he was actually doing other than just… being complimentary. Being kind, as the kids say. She wanted to really know if he felt those things or if he had indeed caught some feelings. She felt possessive and simmering with a quiet rage because of his goddamn nonchalance. Instead, she stoked some other stranger's flames and blew kisses in the dark. Ben didn't have to know *know* about it, but he should at least realize her options were varied. But, that was desperate and undignified behavior. She wanted to stay awake with him, next to him, his head close to her heart and hand on her ass. She wanted to shower with him and smell like his shampoo. She wanted to close her eyes and taste the salt on his skin. She didn't mind surrendering after years of keeping her legs closed and arms crossed.

The ants had come again. They had skittered through the spice rack, and into their kitchen shelves. The mold was looking blacker, her bedroom colder. At the same time, things were looking up. A few hours later, Ben messaged again; she was more playful, teasing, less willing to bend to his mercy. She toyed with his feelings as best as she could, asking him about how he'd feel if she met someone else. Someone who had seen her face and her body. Someone just as unattainable as he was but he'd never know that. He swatted her questions away, nonchalantly asking if she cared about her privacy (she didn't); she asked if he cared she was talking to other guys (he didn't); he asked if she would send him more photographs (she wouldn't); she asked if he could send her one of his face (he wouldn't).

She tried to move on to better horizons. Different horizons at least. A horizon where someone seemed to shower her with compliments in every message, respond statically to every picture. Like Ben had two weeks before. Like he had pretended a few days before. She was fast to excuse his behavior; she couldn't stop thinking about his hair. Long, black and curly. Unfortunately, too similar to someone she'd known as a friend. Now, those black curls seemed to start a fire in her belly, her massive belly.

XVI

BITTERSWEET SYMPHONY

—

Does his leg shake anxiously like hers?

Does he lie on his bed and track the static ceiling with his eyes, thinking about her?

Did he walk into his next class with a smile on his face?

Was he investing as much as she was in whatever they had between them?

Did he care about her at all?

Did he wait, anticipate, their next conversations like she would?

Did he have a laundry list of conversations that he wanted to talk to her about?

Did he think she would like his favorite song?

Would he like hers?

Would he like her if they had met as classmates, as friends, as crushes…?

Would he like her if she changed herself for him?

Catered to his every desire, molded herself into a fair lady, a statue to covet rather than be with?

Had she made him into an ideal? Frozen in an instance of confusion and uncertainty?

He was just a boy, wasn't he?

XVII

"DON'T LET ANYONE CONVINCE YOU THAT PLEASURE IS A SIN."

———

WASHINGTON, 28 MARCH 2020

From: Rumi

Fri, March 28, 10:39 am

hey ANt :)

just wanted to check in w u to see how youre doin
i was biking to class and dedass just realized we havent talked
in like a month LOL
theyre thinking about closing the campus because of covid
anyhoo i know it's not an excuse that i've been kinda distant bc
of classes piling up
 but i hope you know i'm still here for you for whatever.
Lmk if ur free to call sometime ^^

i also realize that its 10:43 so you arent awake

loll nat why does my phone keep correcting you ti ant

Fri, March 28, 2:48 pm

yo

i just got up :]

ty dude

i've kinda been spiraling for the past couple weeks

I like met this guy.

His name is ben and he lives in virginia. i think

actually we havent even swapped face pics yet

wait can yiu call?!

wtfff ok

also did you see that meme i sent you on insta?

hold on ill just send it again

2:54 pm **Incoming Call**

127 min

She had finally spoken to Rumi. And, suddenly, everything was alright in the world. *It was intimidating how much one person can affect life*, she smiled. It was in a good way, every time though. Rumi had convinced her to take a break, to breathe, to ruminate, and to journal. Not to hesitate before taking the plunge into the unknown. Her own instincts of self-preservation were allowed to melt away and she relied on her best friend's instincts. They helped her think through her life objectively. It was a support system she had never had before, even with her mum. She couldn't share certain emotions, desires, as a young woman. She could share her thoughts, opinions, and start never-ending fights with her mum. That wasn't difficult. What was difficult was making up after every stray insult, backhanded compliment, slap-to-the-face mumble. It had gotten tougher over the years to make up; it had gotten easier to say some things, unfair albeit true.

She struggled to resolve her femininity with her mother's, who seemed a forever woman, someone who didn't have to try very hard to be who she was. Someone unlike Nat, in all ways, but someone whose genetic code was so deeply embedded in Natasha. Half of her mum would always exist within her DNA, under her skin, in her thoughts. Her practicality and peace came from her mother. Her rashness and anger, as well as her biting intelligence, from her father. Her sexuality came from within as did her penchant for long-term, deep relationships with friends. Friendship was her rock, through and through. A man couldn't rip that apart. It would never belong to him. Her friendships were her own, hers and her friends'.

Her relationship with Rumi had twisted and knotted into a beautiful evergreen. They'd been through the teenage years, which meant they had essentially encapsulated miniscule versions of a full life between the two of them. Rumi had been with Nat as she had experienced genuine heartbreak, the burn of unrequited loves, the confusion about Nat's own feelings towards people. Everything that made her the person she is today. Rumi had seen it all, and Nat had seen a lot of her best friend's own life. Intimate knowledge strengthened their relationship today rather than create artificial bubbles of jealousies and anxieties as it once had.

It wasn't bad to seek validation from strangers, right? As much as she loved and appreciated Rumi, friends and parents would never see her like a lover—which was good, and healthy. But strangers have their own enticing aura. They didn't really need anything from her, while obviously harboring the desire to fuck her and own her body for a few nights; *those were acceptable feelings for a stranger*, she thought. Transactional, temporary relationships. Though, she'd never want to put a time limit on a sexual encounter. That was a massive turn off. She wanted to fuck him into oblivion… at least, that's what she said to Ben last night, before sending him a virtual good night kiss and turning to her next conversation.

At least with Ben, she had some sense of clarity and reality; he was busy and had a life apart from their shared moments together. He lusted after different parts, more than just her erogenous zones. Ben dreamt of sucking her toes and her newfound confidence let her send several pictures, posing her feet in pretty ways. Suddenly her feet felt sexy, too, and she wanted that feeling to be about her entire body. Entirely.

She wanted men to approach her in public, maybe after she had to bend down to the last shelf in the grocery store. Or when she stretched to retie her ponytail, her breasts straining against her t-shirt. Moments she felt were inappropriate in public, innocent moments for those not watching her lips as the small, satisfied smile appeared after her hair was set back into a ponytail.

She felt overwhelmingly ready yet burdeningly inexperienced. She was ready to break the piggybank of her sexuality and cash in her prize, her long-awaited, desperate prize. Yet, she pulled and held herself back, gave in to strangers online rather than people in front of her. Instead of approaching the beautiful girl she saw in Whole Foods, she buried her face and her life in her phone, waiting for people to like, share, and comment. *And, turn the bell icon for notifications!*

Otherwise, they might miss what this thicc, thicc thot was doing. She sniggered at the nickname and bit her lip in anticipation of her second lover. *I'm a naughty Noughtie.*

Every stranger reminded her a little of Ben, nevertheless. Someone who was anxious, jumpy, shy, and a liar. A pale, dark-haired boy with light eyes. *Nothing like her type at all,* she thought sardonically. She was attracted to the average Joe, but not the name Joe. A white man with dark hair, and beautiful eyes. Eyes that tugged at her heartstrings and hooked onto her navel. Butterflies. Ryan had done that. He had done that so well that she never had the guts to tell him she had liked him for two years. Two painful years of yearning after him, yet not to the point where she submitted her sexual desires to him as well; she dreamed about meeting him later in life and being with him, but it was always more romantic. Ryan was always an ideal, not a possibility.

Women think about sex, too. It was well-documented at this point, but it wasn't hammered enough into the psyches of young teenagers. They needed to learn how to accept their feelings and cherish their desires, explore their wants and needs at their own pace; not have some boy ruin it all in one instant. It happened too much. An image shatters, a heart breaks into a million little pieces, and a girl is left to pick up her life bit by bit before reliving the experience over and over until finding the mystical One.

Why can't there be a Mystical Two? Or a Three? Or Four? Or… Twelve? Who would be lucky number Twelve? The person who sweeps this girl off her feet and holds her close, till death do them part.

Alas, her newest conquest three thousand miles away had slept off. Leaving her high and…wet. She rolled her eyes and focused on her late-night tunes before shooting off a quick 'good night' message to him. Her happy episode had lasted three weeks, and she capitalized on it with the new additions to her playlists. Bouncy, major-key music that sounded like a well-settled teen was writing it. Catchy, and worth several random lazy movements made to the rhythm. Surprisingly, he responded. So, she tied her hair up and got to work.

XVIII

NUMB

—

WASHINGTON, 30 MARCH 2020

That afternoon, I finally liberated myself. I gave in and sent him a full-body pic—like *full*, full-body, fat, hair and all.

My body was my own, but now he held a small part of it in the palm of his hands, seared into his skull; he should have been able to almost feel me under his skin, taste my smile, and hear my laughter. Only a little bit, a small inconsequential piece, a piece I had withheld from everyone else. No one else had this piece, signed and dated from me to him, just for him. I should have felt liberated, I should have felt more excited, thrilled, scared at his reaction. Instead, it fell short of anything I'd felt with him. No navel drop, no butterflies, no endless smile. I felt numb. I didn't care anymore.

Bit by bit, he had already imbibed so much of me, drank in my soul in shot glasses and saw my personality shine through colored lenses. Through him, I sought a salvation, a nirvana, a peak I didn't think existed. Instead, it was mired by curiosity, a fascination, an inquisition rather than a liberation. I felt betrayed by him, and my own emotions. I wanted him to lust after me like a dog in heat, or is that impolite to say? Is it impolite to say that I didn't care if he spread my lewdness across the globe? I didn't care if he kept it all to himself, relishing the pixels on the screen.

Another anonymous encounter had slinked back to the crevice from which he had emerged. The dark romance he had offered so willingly each night seemed to blink away before my eyes. I didn't care about him like that. Maybe I would if I gave him a small chance, but he wasn't honest with me. Ben is honest with me. He was when I asked him outright about his likes and dislikes, his classes… His facelessness made him courageous. It granted him a boon I had never seemed to take advantage of in the past month. Facelessness could be arousing sometimes. I didn't collect faces, I collected memories and people, feelings that burned onto my memory. Emotional, infatuation, transient connections.

People didn't feel pressured to share themselves with me; they wanted to. I still remembered casually talking a man out of his original intention of buttering me up and asking for nudes. I stayed calm and maybe that was the problem: my serenity. I wanted nothing more than the spontaneity of a surreptitious relationship, yet when offered those chances in real life, I shied away from the blinding lights. I felt I would be caught with my pants down, almost literally speaking, but more like halfway out of my bedroom window with car keys in my mouth. Wide eyes, and a costume for a stranger. It sounded risky and foolish. Why meet a stranger now when I could meet someone I see every day? That is, if they have me.

I felt numb because I hyped his reaction up too much. Even though if I had sent myself earlier, I would have felt the immensity of his reaction and his compliments. Instead, I just felt like I was bloodthirsty, power hungry with control over him in some way. And confident in my ability to goad people into interesting situations. Situations, that pants down, I'd never want to be caught in or around.

I'd fallen in love. A comfortable, easy love. A trusting love. I didn't know if I'd ever see him or hear his voice, but I enjoyed his comfort and his company. I liked his presence in my life, and his poorly worded texts, and his copious number of links, and how I could imagine his hair running through my fingers. The curly, black hair that was probably as tangled as mine, shorter if not as dense.

I could picture him sitting and responding to my playful remarks and sarcasm. My high-brow jokes and behaviors dissipated when I spoke to him. With him, I embodied the spirit of another nineteen-year-old boy. Armed with this new information, I wanted to scream at myself for not dropping my standards in college. Why couldn't I just start talking to a stranger? Flirting even, or dating, that horrendous standard. I'd fallen in love with the buzz, not the ups and downs of heavy drinking. Just a cool tipsiness that still prompted me to make the best decisions for myself and protect my heart.

I didn't mind falling in love with him. I didn't feel in love with him; I was infatuated, but warm in the inside. His naivety charmed me, as did his mock-frustration, and clinginess when he had the time. His self-assuredness, and most importantly, his attraction to me didn't hurt any of my own feelings. As much of a self-saboteur I could be, I tried my best not to. Instead, I basked in the numbness' warmth.

XIX

FEET

——

6:07 PM, 4/15/2020
brattypatty is online
brattypatty is typing...
Hey B. Guess what?

8:41 PM, 4/15/2020
tanning.chatum is online
tanning.chatum is typing...
what lol

brattypatty is online

I finally got that nail polish
so...

ooooo nice
is it black

Mhm...

wait
are you wearing it rn

Hmm... I could be

fuuuucccck
thats so hot

;P

duude
stopppp ur sexy ass
righht now
or imma come over there
and fucking rail you

I dare you lol

dont omg
shit
im realllly tireeddd tonight
i cant do anything

Haha, it's ok):
I was getting all dressed up and shit
But who tf cares lmao

awww baby
ill talk to u later ok

Mhm. I'll be here lol

XX

BLACK

—

WASHINGTON, 15 APRIL 2020

I want to feel sexy, Nat thought suddenly, *I want to buy lingerie. If I'm painting my nails black, why should my feet have all the fun?* Ever since she had acknowledged her feelings for Ben two weeks ago, she had tossed everything by the wayside. She needed to resume a routine. Workout four times a week, eat more protein, work on her fat loss. Or she could chuck it down the drain and focus on feeling pretty now. Zapping hairs off her body, wearing No. 5, and letting her hair down. Pulling on a garter, maybe, or wearing crotchless panties or a thong. All so she could enjoy herself, by herself. Feel like being a woman wasn't just about the male gaze, and his eyes on her body. But, also more importantly, her eyes on a mirror and her breath rapidly increasing.

Maybe she could climax without external stimuli.

Maybe she could just drink warm tea and read a book, all while lounging around in real loungewear, not just repurposed cheap dresses.

Better yet, maybe she could take pictures of herself, actually feeling sexy for once. And seek her own validation.

Nat was meant for a wife. She had realized that now; someone to emotionally settle her, someone to cherish and adore her, someone to grow old with, someone to never let go… and all those other pulpy, airport store romance novel titles. Not someone who owned her, but a shareholder of her time and affection. Someone who knew when to back off and when to comfort her. Someone she could spend lazy Sunday mornings with and count the moles on her arms. Someone who indulged her childishness and her severe maturity. Someone she could be there for, even in their silences and time apart. Someone who gave and took as much as she did. Balance.

Honestly, though, she thought, puffing her chest up with air, *I'd be happy with just feeling happy.*

That was what joy was, she mused. Joy was short-term, momentary bliss. Happiness was contentedness, something one felt at all times without effort.

Ben made her joyous, but not effortlessly happy. Their honeymoon period had faded since meeting in February, and unfortunately, all they had were bland texts and one-sided memes. She had to decide how much she wanted him inserted into her life. His curly black hair was just hair again, like his one-worded replies and apathy. He had become distant and she could feel his disinterest stinging her slightly. She wanted to spice things up, paint her nails black, and pretend to strut around her bedroom for him. Even if he was three thousand miles away. Even if it was her birthday in a few weeks.

When, if, she was ever asked where they had met… she'd most likely say Tinder. Or in person, during a debate tournament or collegiate conference. There was no way **The**

Chatroom would be the answer. Even to their kids. If, that is, they had kids. Or a life together, in real life. She was completely open to an entirely online relationship with Ben. He had charmed her that much as to warrant a genuine wireless and atom-less connection. Hell, she was ready to give him her number, but he didn't want to give her his.

While their relationship was mutually beneficial in reducing their loneliness and fulfilling a small portion of their weekly *fuck* quota as virgins, she knew deep down he was giving more than taking. Slowly, cell by cell, he was helping rebuild her self-confidence; that validation, that evolution, was priceless. She felt sexy again, and even if she had traded her heart in exchange, it was worth it. She felt like *herself* again. Like Nat from high school, or Nat before California. He didn't want her heart though, just a few nudes and some type of situation devoid of human emotion. Suddenly, she had become the Iron Throne and he really was Jon Snow with his curly, black hair. He was the one with the orange-and-black links and the "wyd" texts while she was the one with the nudes.

And the one who sends the nudes is making the ultimate internet sacrifice by trusting a faceless, nameless stranger to never leak, share, or doxx her. But Ben had broken down her walls. Faceless as he was, Ben was genuine, sincere, and confusing.

At the end of the day, Nat could only model healthy relationships on the ones she thought were healthy. Her parents were her prime and only example. They embodied that balance, that orbit around each other. It wasn't practical to most relationships, but she understood what made their relationship work. Forgiveness was one of the last tenets she had learned while studying their life together.

Black and brown looked nice, but her tan skin seemed to glow in white. Her nails looked better in white, and even she knew it. It brightened her complexion and brought out the pinkish hues that mixed with the blues of her veins. Black nails made her feel darker, edgier, fifteen again: too young to know what she wanted, too old to be indecisive. White, on the other hand, made her feel maybe a little too preppy and virginal.

At nineteen, she wanted nothing more than indecision, torment, tug-of-war, teasing. But, at least she knew what she wanted. For the moment, at least.

PART III

FANTASIE

XXI

INSOMNIA

She was awake at 4:38 a.m. on a Friday night. Listening to more Frank Ocean and the soundtrack to *Moonlight*. She was in love, she declared silently to herself. She didn't dare speak those words aloud. All that would lead to was unnecessary heartache. Ten more years of it and Ben would become another Ryan. Another martyr in her memory. Instead, she sealed her thoughts in a Ziploc bag and let them squeeze out of a hole the size of a pinprick as she recounted her emotions to Rumi. She was euphoric, again, riding on a wave of another human being this time. Problematic as it was, she liked how he said he loved her (even if it was jokingly, right?) and called her baby. How he didn't care about her that much, but just enough. After a lifetime of mollycoddling by her parents, she could use some roughening up around the edges. Obviously, that didn't mean falling into the arms of a potential manipulator. *But,* she asked herself warily, *Ben can't hurt me from three thousand miles away, right?* Nat was worried for herself and her body. *I don't want a repeat of*—Nat brushed away the thought, that *man,* her breath hitched. The image and perception of her body, and her character that came hitched onto the sidecar of societal judgment.

Bodies. His and hers. Entwined in that sacred embrace they had never expected to be in. A mind fuck. A true, good-new mind fuck. She wasn't sure if he had ever experienced anything like it; she was aroused by the mere mention of sex from him. Or was she just blindsided by her own need to be desired sexually? It was probably a combination of both. An adoration had formed within her, maybe it was one-sided (maybe it wasn't a joke when he said I love you). If anything, the newness had worn off, and while the first few days were incredibly exciting, she was trying to grasp at ways to keep him interested. Painting her toes and lasering her hair, wearing her off-white near-wedding prom dress. All sorts of lazy tricks. She didn't expect herself to concede so quickly. It was probably the lack of action and experience in the last five years; she was not in control of their dynamic. He dictated when he wanted her and when he didn't have time. She was just a piece of meat in more ways than less. A younger version of herself wouldn't have tolerated that; but a fatter, less hairy version appeased those emotions and clung onto his… vibe.

That's what it was, a vibe. The smoothness of jazz or the unsteady hands of a new doctor; this vibe encompassed both feelings. He was nervously in control and dominantly concerned about her feelings. She yearned to compliment him in creative, cute ways, slowly realizing that most compliments fell bare to what he'd refer to her as. In less than seven days, she was putty in his hands and she didn't know how to feel about it between moments of absolute infatuation and love.

And that's also when she had a feeling of déjà vu. For at least four years, since she was fifteen-going-on-sixteen, she'd expected something on Valentine's Day. Whether it was a yes from Liam, or a smile from Brendon, she yearned for romance.

February 14, 2018: she'd started working out after a two-year-long hiatus.

February 14, 2019: she'd booked herself a solo ticket to watch *Isn't It Romantic*. It felt bizarre watching Priyanka on a big screen in the US, surrounded by more white people than desis.

February 14, 2020: she had started speaking to Ben. Her nails had grown. Friendly first, flirty later. He'd made her feel sexy. And she had not expected that to be a Valentine's Day gift.

Nat craved a challenge. She wanted to intellectually spar with her partner, wanted them to make her angry and frustrated, get her blood boiling and get her to say something aggressive with a fire in her eyes. Maybe it was the Leo in her or, more likely, the short-temper and the instant arousal at rage. She wanted to have hot make-up sex and relent to their merciless taunts at losing an argument. Natasha wanted passion, and mania, and intelligence, and teasing. She didn't want only an easy love, or compliments, or heart eye emojis. She'd never realized that one day she could have both if she chose correctly. If it was in her destiny, she had faith that she'd receive that kind of affection and desire. She wanted to experience fire, and what she was receiving with him washed over her like cool water. It made her shiver and thirsty but quenched her need for validation rather than affection. *He's sweet*, she thought, *maybe a bit too sweet.*

I mean, preferring rough sex doesn't make someone... cruel or violent. He's considerate of that; he wants to see me happy too, during our little deaths. Instead, I feel conflicted and torn.

 She wanted him to crave her, but in a good way. She wanted to feel as wanted as she wanted him. *That's it. Isn't that easy?*

Prematurely, she imagined a life with him… four years down the road, they would move cross country together. Eight years, and they'd have a child, or at his pace, three children. She'd recount their story on Ellen's couch to millions of televisions. She'd laugh coyly when asked if they had even seen each other before committing to a relationship. *No, she'd respond, we really didn't need to, you know?* She would have fallen madly, crazily, beautifully in love with him. She would please him at every turn, but only because she'd genuinely want to. He gave her something she had never expected on Valentine's Day: a good *fucking* friend.

A week later, she was content. Perfectly balanced between infatuation and routine. She longed to show herself off but recoiled at the sight of her own body. Eventually, she'd want to change that. She really wanted to change that. Then, during her visit to Rumi's college, she didn't mind meeting someone she could fall in love with, too. In case he fell through—*maybe, he won't*—before then. She felt her period trickle down to her pad and interpreted it as arousal… She was quite aroused nonetheless; he knew which buttons to press in his low-brow sexts, filled with emojis and lacking apostrophes.

Oh, how she desired, she moved, she squirmed, she came, she didn't care. She lost her inhibitions within a week with this man across the country. All she could hope was that he was being honest about who he said he was. Her guarantee to herself was that even if he wasn't, her feelings would only change slightly. She'd still want to see if this odd spark flourished or died in embers. Five years ago, she would have expected herself to be too dedicated to strange men. Here and now, she felt independent. And, sexy. She didn't expect, she demanded, and spoke forthrightly. She teased herself and him playfully, rolling her eyes at his responses while finding specific words oddly triggering. His speech patterns weren't lost on her, and she bought into the image of his age and stature. After all, he teased her right back and she was in awe with certain appendages, too. She pictured him as lean but muscular, pale with long limbs, and curly, black hair. Almost like Prince Eric, to misrepresent *The Little Mermaid*. But she hoped more for Timothée Chalamet, Jon Snow, and of course a young Sirius Black. Hell, if the long hair were sexy, she wouldn't mind it at all. As long as he didn't mind her own hair that grew lonesome on prairies of curved skin, dotted with spots and pores. Her hairs grew fiercely and confidently. They didn't care that most women didn't have chest, stomach, back, leg, arm, facial hair. She was thankful that hair didn't grow on her palms, even though they invaded the backs of her fingers and toes. She would grimace and point them out, but even after years of zapping them off, they kept reappearing like pesky neighbors. If he didn't mind her thousand flaws, she thought she'd like the long hair, and face, no matter what it looked like.

If he delivered on his promises, as she meant to keep hers, who was to say what would happen one day down the road…?

What if he loved me?

What if we got married?

Would I be a good wife?

XXII

NAT / BEN

—

It's our anniversary.

One year into this journey called marriage, and we were living in the same rundown apartment in Chinatown as we did when we first started going out. *Really* going out. When I asked her to move in, Nat just snorted, not bothering to take me seriously. And honestly, I couldn't blame her. I was dead broke; she had just started grad school. It took a whole two days of convincing for her to move just a set of clothes—and then a set of chairs, a coffee table, and her vinyl collection. We were on top of a restaurant-slash-bar-slash-grocers. A little bodega with the incessant scents of General Tso's Chicken and Peking Duck, delicious enough to entice me into a food coma.

Nat has always been so much more thoughtful with her gifts. When she moved in, she brought with her a beautiful set of vintage speakers. After a few hours of fiddling with the settings and position, Nat sat me down on the powdery—"Columbia," she'd like to interject—blue couch and looked me squarely in my eyes. I noticed the beads of sweat dotting her forehead, and swiped at them, my hand staying on her cheek.

"Ben. I want you to *really* listen, okay?" Then, she started playing Miami Sound Machine as if to prove the speakers' mettle. I watched her sway for a couple of minutes, before grabbing her waist and forcing her to sit on my lap. I hummed into her ear, as the auto-play took over as did our bodies.

This year, Nat's gift was a music box playing a vapor-wave cover of my favorite Gloria Estefan song. The song that reminded me of her, back when we were just "talking." That's a euphemistic way to put it; I barely knew what I had gotten into with Natasha. She swept me off my feet, and I think I was able to keep up with her only because *I* became her rock. Someone to keep her grounded while she took on the world. I didn't mind being that for her, because Nat started to mean every-thing to me. *I don't know when she became my world, but I'd like to think it was a slow transition from our "talking" to now.*

I guess it's just emblematic of our relationship. I need her more than she needs me sometimes, or so I think—

"Ben?" I blinked out of my thoughts, to see Nat rushing around in the apartment in a flurry. Her hair's still damp from our shower, and her eyes were frantically searching the living room.

"Yeah, babe. What's up?"

"Have you seen my keys?"

I guess, that's not necessarily always the case. I gestured bemusedly at the TV cabinet. "Do you mean the ones over—"

"Ugh, thank you so much, B." Nat leaned in, and pulled my face closer to hers, before closing the distance. She moved back and wiggled her eyebrows suggestively. "You know I'm not late... yet."

I frowned and nodded towards the clock. "Baby, it's almost nine and you have to take the 1-Train. Your class starts at—"

Nat rolled her eyes and interrupted me with a fiercer kiss. "What were you saying?" I watched as her bag slid from her shoulder and dropped onto the floor with a thud.

She ended up skipping class.

Instead, she chose to lounge around in her underwear after she made us a hearty breakfast and washed the dishes. She even fried up some bacon for me which wouldn't have happened a year ago. *Hm, it really is nice being married.*

As she started reviewing her lesson for the day, I was right on time to start my work: freelance web-developing for a few startups in Brooklyn. My job kept us afloat while Nat finished her last year of grad school. Honestly, I didn't like working as much as I had hoped to when I first started but I'm doing this for both of us. It paid the bills, Nat was focused on school, and we get to enjoy whatever free time she has together.

One year in, and an eternity to go. I can't believe it's already been a year. It feels like yesterday when we were in Hawaii, and I saw Nat become sexier, more confident right in front my eyes. I can't believe this is the woman I'm in love with. This shouldn't have happened. After she accidentally ghosted me, this should *not* have happened. I was so bitter for *months* and then she was the one who found me on Snapchat again. Maybe this isn't a modern-day fairytale, but Nat fought tooth and nail until her parents accepted me, some random guy off the internet. I'm excited for our life. Even with all the crap we had to take from our parents, and that annoying ex of hers (Lamar? Amir?), we're happy. I'm so fucking grateful that she decided to move in with me, and buy us those speakers, and call in a favor on our anniversary.

I can't believe I get to be with the girl of my dreams.

A woman now, who helps me succeed and truly makes me the happiest man in the world.

By being *hers.*

*What if we stayed married
and
he didn't care as much?*

*What if we fell into
complacency and routine?*

What if we weren't made perfectly for each other?

XXIII

HEAVEN OR LAS VEGAS

Mindlessly, Nat thumbed through the mind-numbingly long menu. From Chinese to Mediterranean to Indian, it seemed they hadn't spared a single continent or cuisine of their horrendous cooking. It was eight pages and spanned the length of her forearm. Her eyes glazed over as she turned to the next page. *Of course, they had sushi, too. How inventive.* The plastic cover peeled sadly over some of the stained words, and she grimaced, pressing her hand accidentally against the sticky table. Her stomach turned. *Why had he picked this place?*

He returned from the loo and looked her over appreciatively. "Hey, found anything good yet?" Grinning, Ben sat across her on the puffed red vinyl seat. A low groan released from under him as he settled down, seemingly unaware of the shabby decor and buzzing fluorescent lights. His eyes stayed on the menu, even as she bore holes into his head with a laser. "So...?" He nudged again with the innocent question.

She cleared her throat, and reached for the glass of water, before disgustedly noticing a floating *speck* of something. Her stomach did another somersault, and she felt bile rising slightly. "Benny, why are we here?"

"This is the only place in Vegas that does Indian, babe." Eyes still glued on the second page, he never broke contact. Instead, he reached for her hand and stroked her thumb comfortingly. "At this hour, at least."

Two non-Indian looking servers peered at them from a high counter and spoke to each other in a rapid exchange. The light above them flickered uncertainly.

She drew a breath and hissed. "Ben, I'm not eating here. There is no way in hell I am consuming *anything* from this godforsaken place." Her closed fist involuntarily hit the table as she raised it, and the pain squelched through her arm. She swore and found his eyes on her. Her hand instinctively went to her slightly bulging belly and Ben furrowed his brows at her worriedly.

"Did you just hurt yourself?" Ben winced and pulled her hand closer to him. Taking a deep breath in, he sighed defeatedly. "What do you want to eat instead?"

"I don't know. Shake Shack's still open on the Strip." She raised her brow suggestively and held onto his fingers tightly. "I could *really* use a Shroom Burger…" She paused with bated breath. "And, cheese—okay, no cheese—fries… Maybe a little cheese, just on the si—"

She watched as Ben's face flushed frustratedly. His jaw had locked into that stubborn position, and she could see him swallowing his words. "You know what the doctor said, Nat. No lactose, and especially, no cheese. You've been so good."

Her face fell, and she glanced out of the dust-covered windows at the deserted parking lot. *Why were they in Vegas again? Right, because of the discounted tickets. Who would have thought in less than a year of their marriage, she'd be rearing for motherhood?* Sullenly, she turned back to him, locking eyes and leaning in. "I'm not eating here." She whispered in a low, threatening tone.

His eyes danced as he tried to mask his amusement. Before she could get a sideways word in, he was bellowing over their small table, the booth jostling with his movements. He wordlessly rose from his seat across her—*hrrrummmph*, the seat responded indignantly—and helped her up. Ben put his hands on his wife's waist as he guided them to the door. "We'll be back, guys! Thanks again!" He spoke over his shoulder, at the two servers who hurried back into the kitchen.

The bell on the door tinkled as they exited. Ben walked up to the passenger side, helping her into the seat as she balefully looked at him behind her lashes. He leaned in to buckle her up and kiss her lightly on the nose, before shutting the door. She forced her gaze outside, feeling the car move as he settled into the driver's seat, and placed his hand on the back of her seat to reverse. She could feel his smile on her. His joviality, his amusement with her. She softened and looked back at him, sheepishly. He was chuckling and he brushed playfully against her shoulder, changing gears.

"You alright?"

"I'm alright."

What if I wasn't actually alright and

we aren't meant to be at all?

What if we break up?

Over and over again.

Every night in my dreams?

XXIV

GLASS

———

You know the feeling when you're in the shower. Drenched with water, pelted by the droplets. Like standing directly under the showerhead. The noise is overwhelming, almost overbearing. Deafening.

You can watch as the water glides over your skin. Coating every surface. Suddenly, there's a moment between the pelting and the drying, when your skin glistens, reflects the light almost like a mirror. Your skin looks absolutely perfect, and sometimes it only works on the back of your hand. Which you study and try to recreate every few seconds, because you want to feel perfect forever.

That's how I want someone to love me.

Unflinchingly adore every follicle, every molecule, every bad skin day, every bed-hair day, in halitosis and in health. I want them to see just the perfections within my flaws. Not actually noticing the details, the subtext, the underlying tension in my behaviors and mannerisms. The clenched jaw, the through-the-teeth smile, the fear in my eyes. Because, as unfortunate as it is, I'm always terrified.

Terrified that someone will find me out as an imposter, a poser, someone will call my bluff, call me a fraud.

Terrified that I have no real future with them whatsoever and terrified they think I'm their backup, their second-best plan, their second-best lay. Their second-best life.

If someone sees me for all my perfections while ignoring my flaws, implying I have flaws that they have to ignore pointedly, is it even worth being with them? Someone who ignores my short temper, my laziness, my prejudices, my lies, my brutality. I wouldn't kill a butterfly, but I kill ants and spiders mercilessly, but not guiltlessly. Before I squash them between my forefinger and thumb, I used to get a tinge of guilt, pity, a sinking feeling in my heart that I was so bothered by a creature 1/1000th my size. Maybe even smaller, maybe I'm more vicious than I thought.

But, that's not possible. The water can't always flow and coat my body. My imperfections can't always hide, and once they stop hiding, what'll he do? Will he leave? As my skin dries and my flaky pores are revealed, will he recoil in repulsion? Refuse to look me in the eyes? Drive away late into the night, with his suitcase packed and his toothbrush in the bin? Will I run after him, try to cajole and coerce him back into the house, into my life? Even when he so desperately tried to leave?

Isn't that what I did last November? Eight days after his birthday. I giggled and joked with the kids before cornering him into a fight. A full-on shit show that ended with him leaving, fuming, not even waiting for me to run out the door and shout his name into the night.

Ben. I would have shouted helplessly to that darkness if I had bothered to leave our foyer.

Bothered to stand in the freezing New York snow, wrapped in a thin robe, shivering at our doorstep, watching my breath frost up. *Ben, please come back inside so we can talk.* Talk, as if it were so easy when he would never listen, when I'd have to dumb myself down, slow my brain to a spluttering, hiccupping halt and start moving my lips slowly, monotonously, bitterly. I hated how I was smarter than him, in more ways than I used to think.

How I was genuinely leagues above him in some ways, but how I stuck around. How I had refused to have a third kid. How I had slept in the basement that night, not even having the desire to make up with him.

Even after hearing the stairs creak under his weight, and the door to our bedroom being locked. How he had switched on his hard-rock playlist on the speaker. How he had grunted when our daughter asked him to read her a bedtime story. How he had slammed the bathroom door. How he had stopped at the top of the basement stairs for a solid minute before… walking back upstairs. Into our bedroom. Sitting on our bed and switching off the lights.

And, essentially, telling me and my pride to fuck off for a night. Rightfully so, I may add. Since that was the just the first of many nights I slept downstairs in the basement, listening to him toss and turn on our squeaky mattress.

XXV

I OWN MYSELF

—

Her wrists, my hands, her feet, my curls and ripples, her hair, my face, her anger, my smile, her toes, my eyes.

Relentless eyes.

Sad eyes.

Dead eyes, glassy so they reflect the flickers of light shined on them.

They retract the colors they hate and absorb the ones they love.

The reds, the yellows, the green speckled with gold, and the black.

The deepest, darkest blacks. Black enough to stay after all the colors disappear.

Tangled hair. Messy, with a side of greasy. Old, depression hair. Dreadlocked from sleep, bleached by the heat. Noisy, ruddy, black hair that sits atop a long, dotted forehead and those restless eyes. And a duplicate nose. Lips that seem to run for miles and a starlet chin.

The droplets of sweat that appear on my forehead, and trickle down the back of my neck.

The shivers and hot flashes.

The blushes and the stares.

I own only myself, and no one can own me.

I am but a piece of art, on display in a museum; people can stare, snigger, laugh, and judge, but they can never share my emotions. They can touch me and feel the weight of my soul in their arms, so heavy that it nearly touches the ground. So heavy it sinks onto itself, bending and folding, until it collapses like a boneless arm.

I own a soul so heavy that it will need lifetimes to heal.

Lifetimes to change and reveal the things I cherish. The small brushes against my fingertips and the heat underneath my skin, a soul that isn't protected by anonymous whims. A heart that has caged itself for protection, locked away for an eternal affection.

My heart, that beats to the drum of a new rhythm, hopes to change every season. A dusty space between my ribs, held together by a thread of flesh and affliction. A bubbling anger that never seemed to penetrate the surface of her being, but stayed, seething, boiling, churning, until every once in a while it bursts and leaps in bounds and seizures.

She collects herself before leaving the room angrily. She doesn't know why she's so angry, so afraid of these feelings.

She's afraid of herself and what she'd do to anybody who came in her way.

Afraid of the violence embedded in her DNA. Her genes that shouldn't have existed, resisted the changes when they were made. The rites of passage her ancestors took, the oaths to gods and goddesses unknown; to kings and paupers, both. Her misinformed machismo, her swagger, the crispness of her tongue and the dull lack of emotion.

She had devolved into a machine of her own making, a woman unkind.

Ownership never ceased, when it was in reference to her dreams.

Her ambitions, her miseries, she expected them all to coexist with ease. Pulling them apart, teeth by teeth, she analyzed and reanalyzed until she needed a break.

Her personality would not define her. Her aggression was only in part, and her compassion was greater.

Right?

The fire in her voice, while temporary, would burn onto the minds of others. She breathed through her pain and expected to disappear without much effort.

Her pain, manifested in headache after headache, argument after argument, heartbreak after heartbreak, only to end in a numbness of all emotion.

Devoid of feeling, how would she experience her pain?

Would she ever have to grit her teeth, or glare, or snarl, or smirk, or hit, or scream?

Would she ever have enough time to gnash her jaw and speak?

Yes, she would. *How else would they feel* her *ache?*

XXVI

HER

—

"Hey, B. I just wanted to call and say I love you and I miss you... and, I can't wait until you get back home on Saturday..." Nat paused with a smile.

"I stayed up till 2 a.m. again. So I could talk to you. You said, you'd be up at five, right? But, then, uh, you texted to tell me that you were busy. So... I guess, I'm leaving this thicc-ass voice memo."

(Huh... I guess, no matter what I think, I'm still a child in all of these bits, huh? *Thicc-ass,* **my ass.)**

"Does that make me desperate?"

"Actually, don't answer that. I don't think I could handle it if you said yes." She sniggered lightly, pressing the phone closer to her ear. "Fuck it, I'll be desperate."

"I adore what you say, you know, Benny. Honestly, unless you neg me to death, only then I'd start to not give a fuck... But, when everything you say is so sweet, so fucking pure that it makes me a puddle of hot chocolate with cinnamon. Though, I'm pretty sure I'm allergic to cinnamon. I've told you that, right—"

(Hm... I told him last night, didn't I? Is that why this is on my mind? Or is it because of the YouTube rabbit hole of old cinnamon challenge videos?)

"Okay, anyway, I can't believe we're getting married next month." The sound of liquid being poured from a bottle gave Nat a moment.

(Wait. What am I drinking? Am I drinking *drinking*? Like, is that red wine...? Whose idea was that?!)

"I also wanted to say how much I love you for being such a sweetheart. I just want to feel accepted and somewhat cared for; you gave me that. Sorry, give. That's all I asked for at the end of the day," she chuckled, sipping.

"I can't live without our conversations, babe. I have to pull my phone out of my pocket every three minutes to check whether you've sent me anything. Like, literally, every three minutes." She could hear her smile as she spoke, her cheeks were starting to hurt.

(God, I think I'm a gen-you-ine simp. This is it, folks, this is how he becomes the only person in my life. This is what Rumi warned me would happen.)

"I don't think I've ever felt that way about someone. I know, I know, you don't like phone calls, so I'm not calling. Compromises, right?"

(Nope. Now I know. I have simped. This is my simp life. Eventually, I will become a meme and lose all sense of reality.)

"And, before you jump to any conclusions. No, I'm not breaking up with you. I'm just bored. To death." There was a long sigh and an even longer pour. "And no, I didn't cheat either."

"Did you?"

"Kidding… Kidding… I guess, you must be really fucking busy in New York since, well, you've ignored my texts for three days." There was an edge in her voice that she didn't realize was there.

"You know what, I'm sorry. It's just that I haven't spoken to you in… Well, ages. And, because I care so much about you. Honestly, I really, really—love—never mind."

"Why do you hate when I say I love you, again? Like, you find it weird or—whatever."

(Oooh, honey. That is a red flag. That is one big fucking red flag. This isn't really Ben, though, is it? Like, this is just not him… But, hold up, how do I know what he's like?)

"How was work again? I hope your boss liked his gift. At least you're getting somewhere with him… Somewhere close to a promotion, maybe…? Maybe before we get marri—again, sorry to nag."

"Anyway…" She dragged out the word, and took another sip, swishing the liquid around. "Your birthday's coming up… What do you want?"

"Or it could be the same gift as last year… You wouldn't mind that would you…" Nat chuckled, hesitantly continuing.

(Wow, a simp and a hoe. I've come full circle. Jesus Christ, when will the painful shit end?! Why can't I hear myself? He's so obviously a giant asshole!)

"Not like I felt like a whore or anything with your name on my ass…"

(Are you fucking kidding me?!)

Her phone pinged, and she touched the notification. Ben had been tagged in… with *that* girl. They had dated, hadn't they? For a couple months, after… after Nat had called it off a year into their relationship. She always trusted that he hadn't fucked around with that other girl after they got back together—

"Oh, what the *fuck*. Are you fucking kidding me, Ben?! You're busy tonight because you've been with... What's her face?!"

(ARE YOU FUCKING KIDDING ME?!)

"Madison. Right."

"Goddamnit…" She let out a bitter chuckle, scrolling through the comments and back up to the picture. Madison had a hand on his leg, and he was grinning broadly. "Please tell me you just went to dinner. Wait, is—is her hand on your thigh?"

Squinting and scowling, Nat gulped from the glass again.

(Take it easy, fake-Nat. You're probably a lightweight. I'm probably a lightweight.)

"Can we at least talk about what happened… when you thought *I was fucking around*? I've never hung out with him, so I don't even know what's up your ass about *him*." She could feel hot tears pool and threaten to spill. With a shaky breath in, she apologized slowly.

(Wait—)

"Sorry. I'm sorry."

(What the fuck?!—)

"Actually."

(Oh my—)

"I'm not. I should go… "

(Oh. My. God. Is this our breakup? Are we—)

"Whatever. Don't try to save this, *baby*..."

(Damn, girl. Go. Off.)

"I'm—I can't fuck with this anymore. Fuck, Benny, I ignored you sleeping around because I didn't care if you had sex with someone else. You just told me about it... but...

you guys were in love, it felt like that at least. At least to me. And, seriously. It's been three days, and you haven't even—," Nat slurred her words, slightly hiccupping through the tears.

(You little lightweight bitch. Wait—sleeping around?! Why would you do that to yourself, Nat? Why would I... I should just see where this goes, then.)

"You left me, you fucking abandoned me here, Benny. And, I'm supposed to be supporting you and your fucking career? I'm alone in LA, Ben. What the fuck am I supposed to do now?! Catch the next flight out for *you*?! What have you ever done for *us*?! When was the last time you said you loved me, Ben? I get it, that you're frustrated that I can't move just yet and I can't—fuck!"

She slammed her fragile glass down on the counter, furiously, inadvertently. It fragmented into several pieces, over the kitchen's hardwood and into the sink. *Fuck*, she thought helplessly, moving gingerly in her seat. She could see a little blood on her hand, from where the glass had cut, and felt herself wanting to keep talking.

"At the e-end of the day, Ben." She stuttered slightly. "I am my own person. I own my person. I can't be *yours all the time*. Especially when you're not here, ever, for me. I don't know why we're supposed to get married. Like, were we ever... even going to? What the fuck were we thinking..."

"Yeah, I guess... uh, I don't think we're meant to be together. That means, I'm not ready for you and your passiveness or whatever. And, your stupid indecision. I always worried that I was too fast for you, that you couldn't keep up. And, I guess, maybe I just couldn't slow down so much. Maybe, that's enough of a reason to—"

"I need to stay in LA, Benny. I need to *not* wait around for you to call, and to go to sleep and to feel confident," her voice broke, as she stuck her jaw in place and soldiered on, "in us and our ability to work together. Like a couple should. Like I—"

"Bye. Don't... call back at least not until you reach LAX. I can't listen to your voice, right now, like—I'll be gone for a couple of days, okay? I think I need to go to my parents' place. Um. I'll let you know when I'm leaving. It'll probably be before you come back home anyway."

(Oh...)

"And, I'll leave the ring, okay. Just. And, the dress, and the keys. Um. I—"

(Oh.)

Nat faltered, confused, conflicted. Slightly annoyed at her anger and her aggression. Her impulsion.

(Hm...)

"Just... Take care, Ben."

Pressing the little upward-pointing blue arrow, she swallowed and turned her attention to the scene in front of her. Blood was seeping through the hem of her sleeve now, in little dredges, and she could see the glass reflecting off the hardwood. Twinkling at her, mocking her frustration. Nat groaned, and buried her head in her arms, letting out a throaty sob and allowing herself to grieve for a minute before starting to pick up the biggest pieces.

What if it ended tomorrow?

What if I left him?

What if he ended up with
somebody else
prettier than me?

XXVII

HIM

He watched as she bent down to the last drawer. The honeymoon lingerie still looked good on her, leaving very little to the imagination, even if it wasn't anything he'd not already seen before. It was in black, his favorite color on her, with accents in red, her favorite color. It represented a compromise of sorts. The compromise that had guaranteed eight happy years together.

(Eight... eight... Why eight? Eight *is* important. Twenty-eight is the age mummy and daddy got married, so, here I am, with a man for almost a decade. At twenty-eight. Literally, what is wrong with my brain?! Okay. Valid... I should paint my nails black.)

(Hey Siri, can you set a reminder to... Paint. My. Nails.)
(Okay, Nat. I've set a reminder to "Paint my nails")
(Thanks, Siri...)

That was about to end, he sensed earlier in the day when she assaulted him with a barrage of kisses and ushered the kids into her parents' car. There was a flurry, an urgency, in how she had embraced him and enticed him upstairs. The playfulness was now gone, but he could still feel her warmth on the sheets and in the ambiance. She was still in love with him, he realized every now and then. Their two children, a girl and a boy, helped them stay together, as unfortunate as that was. And, while they were never on the verge of divorce, that compromise had eroded. He had become enamored with his lifestyle and she was weighed down by her own career.

She was not his dream girl. Far from it really, she'd entered his life suddenly when they bumped into each other. It was a whirlwind romance, but he'd never expected himself to fall in love with a woman like her. Career-oriented, athletic, blonde, and serious.

(Wait, wait, wait... this is my fantasy. Why am I blonde? Why am I *not* his wife? Why is the girl Ben ends up with... Oh. *Oh*. I'm not her. That isn't me, is it?)

She dated to marry and nothing less than that was acceptable. She'd only had two other boyfriends before his drink spilled on her and they'd laughed their way through seven years of marriage. Lucky number seven.

Eyes still focused on his soon-to-be ex-wife, he inhaled deeply and tasted the last few moments they'd shared before speaking. "What is this all about?"

"What do you mean?" She stopped rummaging in the drawer for a split-second, before continuing without hesitation. "It's Valentine's Day! I thought we deserved some time off..." She spun around and the image of her stapled itself in his mind. She looked tiredly beautiful; her hair was in slight disarray and she hadn't covered herself up. Her robe was balanced precariously on her forearm.

He swallowed. "I know about the posting."

A blink, a moment of terse hesitation before she cleared her throat. "Babe, I didn't mean for you to find it. Like, the letter just showed up and—" She looked at him ashamedly. "I haven't fully processed it either. And, I can dispute it. They know I have a family a-and…" Trailing off, she pulled on the robe, not bothering to close it, before slinking into bed.

(Damn, son. He's a real pain in the ass, isn't he? She's out there trying and shit, and instead, *he* thinks it's her fault?! Wait. Did I accidentally make her a military woman? Or, what else posts you… um, is she in consulting? Is that even what consultants do?)

Long distance had ruined their relationship once before and he wasn't ready for that to happen again. They had almost ended things until she had made a surprise trip home and immediately got pregnant with their son. Their marriage was already starting to crumble when their daughter was born three years ago. Yet, it was enough for them to stick it through for a few more years. Becoming a father had changed him profoundly for the better. He had even started working remotely a few months after their son's birth; he quickly became their children's primary caregiver. And, in less than six years, their marriage disintegrated. It was mutual; he was tired and so was she. Their marriage had become a spectacle performed for the kids and his wife's parents.

(Of course, he's a good dad. I always feel like he'd be a great dad… Like, a really nice, reliable father. Fuck, this is just going to break my heart more, isn't it? Realizing this will never be *our* future together?)

They sat silently, fingers laced together. "We can't do this again, can we?" Feeling her nod against his shoulder, he shut his eyes and breathed in.

What if I was only a dream for him?

What if we never met?

What if he were only a dream?

XXVIII

NAT // BEN

—

NAT

I'm lying here thinking of you, Ben.

Thinking of you in my dreams.

I know I'm here

In bed, next to someone else.

I know I'm not there

In the passenger seat of your car, on a late-night run to Taco Bell.

I'm sorry I made a fool of you, B.

I'm so sorry, that I kept conflating my feelings for you as feelings of validation for myself.

I'm so sorry I left you on read.

I really thought you would wait. At least a moment,

Or a day, or maybe three.

I don't know if I broke your heart or my own.

I'm so sorry, Ben.

You were so kind and natural.

You were so open. But you hated when I was.

You hated when I tried,

To paint my nails white

Not black like the image in your head.

Of me in bed.

I'm so sorry that I hurt you.

She made a fool of you, but you made a fool of me, too.

I don't know why there are tears in my eyes.

I thought I was over you, and our butterflies.

I still want to know what it feels like to hold your body,
rather than his. Does that make me a bad person? To run
your hair between my fingers and sigh.

Don't… don't bother to answer. I know you can't.

I cut my losses and ran.

I'm twenty now, mature and easy.

Easy to see and be with.

Easier only because of you, Benny boy,

and I might forget that.

BEN

Uh oh,

I don't know why you did that. I don't fucking understand
how you could just ghost me like that.

So, I blocked you.

I know you might be mad, big mad—but, I won't be back. I
can guarantee you that. I'll live somewhere between your
ribs and the space between your ears, you call a mind.

I liked you in my life.

Why did you stop being so easy?

So easy to include in my daily life, my classes, my playlist,
and in my list of contacts.

I liked you in my life.

When did you realize that it wasn't enough?

Not enough to just have you in my phone, and not always
in my head. In my body, but in my zone. And, not in my
heart. Not really.

I liked you in my life.

When did you realize I couldn't love, not after what she did
to me?

What gave you the right to leave me?

What gave you the right to ghost me?

What gave you the right to cease and desist

Our -ship.

You did ghost me, you know, you bitch.

So much for our late-night conversations and heartfelt
preferences for adult websites.

So much for our chemistry.

Which I guess we never had, if you deem it so.

Why did I use the word deem?

Because you're in my dream, Nat.

You'll always be a dream, Ben.

Yet you still fell in love with me.

XXIX

I AM NOT A PERSON

I am not a person. I am a feeling. I am a muse for my own senses. I am a body floating a thousand miles per second around a dying star. I am one with the universe. I am one with myself and a God that needs no remembrance. I will love and I will live. I will live to love and one day, I will find someone who lives to love me, too. Someone who didn't shelter me in a cocoon for nine months or bear the seeds of my existence.

I am not a person. I am a thread of nirvana strung through the beads of time. A gothic manifestation of a bygone era wrapped in vellum and gauze. Sheltered and wombed in the Mother's embrace.

One day, I will find myself, a body floating a thousand miles around the universe. Jettisoning into the abyss that is my mind. Anchoring onto the only reality I know, a reality unknown. I am a body. I am a soul. I am a life. I can breathe in and out and create existence. That is my power, that is my strength. That is my body. Breath in and breath out.

I will become a person. A person full of ambition and hopes and dreams and other people. Little people who belong to me and my dreams. I will into existence whatever I know and whatever I do not will remain, embedded in the grey folds between my eyes. Everyone else can fade away and I'll dance on the ground from which I sprung.

I am only a body. My soul will never cease to exist. I will live eternally in heaven's arms, on the lap of my gods, resting easy until I save myself. I will exit this cycle, in one lifetime or many. I will leave this realm of being to join another one. My feet will dance on the bodies of others. I will take what I need without guilt. I will become someone more than who I am. My confidence will take flight one of these days. It was whispered to me over nine months, sheltered in my mother's womb. I'm a goddess, a partial goddess, a little bit of a goddess. Enough so that I'm not godless and will never be a headless chicken.

I am a purpose.

I just don't know what yet. Time will tell me, they say, time will guarantee I won't waste my time on Earth. One day, my feet won't touch the ground.

I am a frenzy.

I am a whirlwind, a wheel spinning cotton. Yards and yards, until it draped across the sky and over the Earth. Cotton clouds and candy skies. My mind races besides me, my fingers too weak to complete me. My life too young to see beyond a week. My heart beats in a two-step I can't keep pace with. Breath in and breath out. My lungs balloon and then constrict. Suddenly, I'm not breathing.

I am a body.

What if I dreamed and dreamed

and forgot he was a real person?

What if that's the best way to be?

*Suspended in a moment of
my memory's fanfiction*

XXX

IMY

—

12:37 PM, 5/6/2020

tanning.chatum is online

tanning.chatum is typing…

brattypatty is online

heyy

brattypatty is typing…

Hey :)

wyd

Nm lol
Wbu?

same haha

my phone is still broke as fucccccc

Aww damn /:

When are you getting a new one?

idk
whenever this whole pandemic shit is over

Oof. That's gonna take a while...

yeah fuck corona

Haha, yeah!

anyway i'm on my laptop rn
and it's super slow
and i've been hella bussy with classes
so
like
don't hate me ok

Lmao, I won't...
How are classes?

shit
duuuude
lmy

I miss you too <.<
sry for bein a simp yike

i wanna fuck you
so bad but like
i have no time

Hmm… that sucks… ///:
well why don't you in any case????

well
then
tonight
were boutta
do some
nasssssssty shit

Oh, yeah…? ^_~
Like what?

bitch pls
imma fuck the shit outta u
just wait until tonite

Aight, B
Just fucking be on time LMAOOOO

stfu
i'm super busy
i miss ur sexy ass

<.<

Something had changed. He minded her hair, it seemed, and her stretchmarks and her spots. Maybe it was how he was writing the same meaningless nothings and how he had stopped whispering about the sanctity of their relationship. Maybe it was the way he whined more and then never responded for hours. Or how he asked her to do things she wasn't completely sure about. She began to feel the cracks in their foundation. They met when she was in her prime of the month, her body rearing for motherhood, in anticipation for sex. Yet, here she was barely three months later, feeling an unknown detachment. Maybe it was how he feigned interest or didn't engage in invigorating conversations. How she had to lead while he followed, albeit slowly and hesitantly. How she wanted to please him, appease him, paint her nails and primp. Make rash monetary decisions to grasp at the empty air he occupied next to her while he was thousands of miles away.

So she looked. Well, her past self did. She had found people—men—willing to put up with her coyness and her wit. One who complemented her lips. One who laughed at the end of her fingertips. One who merely enjoyed her company. And one who tried forcing her into submitting. She didn't. She'd dissuade and sway, lingering on the words before saying them. Pursing her lips in preparation. Making gestures in front of her and recoiling at their suggestions.

Maybe when she felt better she could persuade herself to drive her car to someplace safe and enjoy a first date.

Shit. It was coming over her, a fast panic ready to trigger an implosion of the senses. She curled onto her side, and felt her face contort into an unseen monster. She buried her head in the small of a pillow and forced deep breaths in and out of her body. Her toes lost their feeling as they explored the frozen depths beneath her duvet cover. *Momentary bliss would return soon*, she guessed. *Not soon enough*, she knew, *but with enough practice it wouldn't feel momentary.* She had a goal to achieve and she wasn't going to let her self-doubt stop herself. Instead, she'd power through her existence like a hydraulic press on apples. Squeezed to the nth degree, but still brittle and fibrous, tough to digest. Like eating raw cud from a pasture. Or reliving old insecurities and letting the new ones hide behind her mask of fragility.

Here lay Natasha. Despondent again.

In her mind, she imagined faceless bodies holding her and caressing her tresses. Legs wrapping around her and pulling her into embraces. She imagined her laugh, next to theirs, and exhaled painfully. She couldn't. All she could think of was her impending doom. Her bare shoulders, chapped lips, and cold feet. All the cold feet. Her stomach heaved, it had its own ecosystem of hair, skin and stretchmarks. She'd ignored it for so long that it had grown ten-fold before she started to pay attention. She hoped whoever chose to sleep next to her would too. *Ignorant bliss was the best*, she reaffirmed. Even if it meant forgetting all she didn't know. That was the important part. She had to forget she ever existed like this, she had to let her insecurities seep through any decorum, she had to become colder or ignore people, she had to rely on herself. The switch was almost instantaneous. Three months this lapse in judgment had lasted. She wouldn't reach out unless he did. She wouldn't cry spent tears. She'd lock her jaw stiffly and feel her hairs chafe her neck. Holding some weight in her heart, she restored her balance in a way. The knot in her stomach returned, her playfulness disappeared, her mood soured, and she allowed herself to lose herself in her music again. She inhaled again, feeling her ribs press uncomfortably on her heart and the violent shaking of her leg.

What more do you want? She wanted to ask herself. *You can't keep doing this every month. Your life is more than these spells, and these episodes. Just because you don't feel them as much as other people doesn't mean it's not important to acknowledge.*

My life.

Do I still own it? Is it mine to behold or another's? Am I allowed to turn my world upside down? Am I allowed to turn the hourglass that falls every three weeks? Am I allowed to sleep and eat my feelings away? Am I allowed to lie to my parents? How do I feel about that? Is it completely negative?

Do I feel left behind? Yes.

Did I leave myself behind? Yes.

Did I betray my past self by trusting life to happen to me rather than making the best of my life? Absolutely. Undoubtedly. Unabashedly. Yes.

At least "The Twenty-Year-Old Virgin" doesn't have the same ring to it as "The Forty-Year-Old Virgin," even if I have to go through the same hair removal process on my mons pubis. All I can do now is wipe away my sleep and tears and feel the growing beard pierce my chest uncomfortably. Facial hair dotted my chin sparsely yet boldly; black and thick, each hair stood erect.

She wanted someone to appreciate her long eyelashes, her laugh, her warmth, her enthusiasm, her being, her gross habits, her hair, her clogged pores and her stress-suscepti-ble skin. Her hands and nails, her hidden oddities, the ones people assumed were anal quirks. She wanted, desired, and lusted after an expired image of her ideal lover. She pictured the silhouette of a boy she once knew, or the superimposed snapshots of boys she knew, muddled into one unattainable idea. She only ever thought of men; maybe this affirmed her heterosexuality. Yet, she never imagined growing old with a man. Now, the present mattered more, and she realized by interacting with men solely she'd learn why she wanted her life-partner not to be one. Men could be predatory, and manipulative, and terrifying—but so could she. How many times had she ended it with Ben in her head over the course of a month? Why did she want him to give up on her so badly? The conflict consumed her thoughts and her deep breaths turned into shallow sighs as she explored the folds of grey matter instigating these feelings upon her.

PART IV

BOMBAYWALLA

XXXI

BOREDOM

———

WASHINGTON, 12 MAY 2020

Things were fizzling out with Ben. To a nearly flat, opened two-liter bottle of soda. Nonexistent

bubbles tittered on either side of the plastic, and instead of crescendoing, dropped to a dull hum of pops. It had taken barely three months. What a pathetically short time to stop feeling, lusting, loving. Fizzled out was maybe a little dramatic. They still spoke and exchanged messages every day, but they were different. More platonic, more quotidian. Less sexually charged, less like Ben from her dreams. Like the Ben she had dreamed about. The Bens she had made, dated, and broken up with in her mind for the past month. She still loved him, but it was less bubble and more sugary caramel-colored liquid.

But Nat was still feeling herself tonight. With a lazy smile, she posted an obvious thirst trap, waiting for the bees to come knocking in her DMs for her honey. Nat promised a fun, no strings attached conversation, even if lackluster towards the end. Instead of her usual approach, she sat on full display and waited for the good few to rise to the top of her chats.

That's how Nat met Omar.

What started as a casual exchange of jokes and a quick mutual realization about their shared ethnicity, devolved into something more primal, more internet circa 2000s. She was curled up in her living room, watching a film with her mother, something dumb and mindless. On her sticky couch, leaning her head against the wall and looking down at her phone through her lashes. She gave in to his charm a little bit, she felt a bit pressured but only because he threatened to leave the conversation. She was rash, and tired. It had been a long day, and suddenly she was confronted by this humorous, Hindi-speaking specimen of a man. She was oddly entranced by his quadruple texting and slow internet—which basically meant they spoke to each other quickly, within the same minute, an unusual occurrence in today's smartphone etiquette between strangers. Lost between the film playing on the television and her mother's interjections, Nat started typing more frantically.

He was lonely. So was she.

He wanted to meet. She wanted to stay in the comfort of her own home and in her ratty pyjamas.

She wanted him to text her; she sensed an underlying sincerity from him that he'd soon blow to bits.

He refused to send a picture of himself. She sent two, both a bit more teasing than she'd have preferred.

He complimented her breasts and she squirmed. It wasn't a bad compliment at all, just unexpected.

He complained that he couldn't have her calling him brother—*bhai*—and then baby in the same sentence. While Ben understood the intricacies of their shared Gen Z lingo, Omar didn't.

He said he dreamed of New York; she dreamed of LA.

When she mentioned her South Indian background, he immediately replied that it was a turn off. Maybe that's what prompted her to prove him wrong.

It was a haphazard frenzy of photos and illiterate bilingual dialogue, tangled in a mess of social awkwardness and her tenacious punny humor. He didn't understand her sometimes, especially during her best jokes, and that frustrated her.

Omar was sometimes sweeter than Ben and he said the right things, maybe just not at the right time. He tugged on her heartstrings and made her blush, made her feel like a hook was pulling her navel into itself and deep into herself. It was an addictive dopamine hit. She liked it, she liked what it did to her internally. But, Omar didn't have the same instant lustful frenzy effect she'd experience talking to her dark curly-haired one. He was obvious in his desires but vague in his language. A theoretical lover in some ways, disparate from Ben, who she agreed would fuck her into oblivion.

However, when she swiped between her spread legs, Nat was surprised at his effect. Sweet or not, Omar still toyed with her sexually, pleasantly even. He showered her with a thousand virtual kisses and took his slow, sweet time. *It was almost romantic,* she smirked, unlike… her mind wandered to those curly black locks and she snapped out of it. Ben was just as nonexistent as Omar, but she was locked into Ben for some unfathomable reason. She wanted him more than he did her, or so she imagined. She never thought he would appreciate her for her mind or her wit or her charm. Maybe just her ass and titties, as he would call them so eloquently. Juvenile, almost, too young to care for a woman in a genuine way. Too young to understand that her body parts weren't on sale, but her heart was in clearance.

Back to Omar, her temporary one, who she had barely spoken to... Who she barely knew or understood. Still, Omar suggested they meet over text. She declined as sweetly as she could; she wasn't ready for that, she still lived with her parents, she'd feel awkward lying to them or sneaking away in a stranger's car. Truth is, she lived in Washington State. Home of Ted Bundy and the Green River Killer, so people shouldn't be as surprised as they usually are when she refused their invitation to meet-up in the middle of the night. There was an impenetrable tension between them. She was afraid she might set him off, and that he may leak whatever she sent him, faceless or not. He was risky, interning at her dad's workplace, and possibly even knowing her dad. He was a twenty-minute 520 drive away. Too close. That was the most terrifying thought: everything being disastrously revealed too early and her whole plan for enjoying her time off going caput.

This was what ended the conversation. His desire to meet her, touch her, and then fuck her.

It was so simple and too easy that she decided against it. As though there was another choice. Staying in her comfort zone, her loose pyjamas, and in her own bed, sounded like the best way to spend her free time. He insisted on meeting tomorrow. Then, as the conversation reached its climax—as did he—Omar nudged again. This time, she waned. Maybe it was time to meet him; screw it, he had way too many identifiable details, he could go public with any of her pictures, her face, her flirtations. Why didn't the risk thrill her?

Boredom. Ben, too busy to respond, too noncommittal to suggest anything more. Her string of anonymous texters, barely showing their faces, or revealing their intentions. And Omar, this new one, who went from hot to cold in mere

seconds when he didn't get what he wanted in such an obnoxiously boyish way she was reminded of Ben.

The bad aftertaste lingered in her mind as she bid him
goodnight and switched off her phone frustratedly. This
dynamic was going to cause her a lot of pain one day, and she
was annoyed at herself for putting her body in that situation.

XXXII

MODESTY

—

While flipping through the stack of tween-aimed magazines, Nat once saw a cartoon graphic of an adolescent girl brushing her teeth with her shirt off. In the mirror, she was supposed to have noticed her breasts developing. If Nat were brushing her teeth like that, all she would have noticed were here discolored armpits—dark enough to never want to raise her hand too high in class, afraid of sweat stains or ever wearing something sleeveless. It was the oddest sight: why on earth is that girl's shirt off? What business does she have looking at herself naked, so brazenly?

You see, an Indian woman is given the gift of modesty, handed down through generations of matriarchal lineage, through hushed tones and stern glances.

An Indian woman is not supposed to see herself sexually. If she does, she risks that sexuality oozing and leaving the essence of her being. If she does, she can be branded a common whore and get what she deserves in the back of a bus.

No, for an Indian woman, her modesty is her dignity.

Her dignity rests on her shoulders and hangs between her breasts to cover up her cleavage in a *dupatta*; her dignity is pinning the *palloo* of her sari to her cotton blouse;

wearing a petticoat, and holding her hand to her chest when she bows. Her dignity lies between her legs for no one to see, to hear, to touch. Not even herself. Her dignity is shrouded by the unclean sanitary pads hanging off of a secret balcony. A locked door to bar entry. Her dignity is mauled by soft touches and tugs, accidental gropes and brushes, the sight of a dick in a man's hand as he pees.

For an Indian woman, her dignity is not hers but her family's.

Her dignity is risking rape as she shits in the middle of a field, surrounded by other women risking their own bodies. Her dignity is tangled up in five thousand years of tradition that connects power and strength to femininity. Her dignity is the trident in her hands, and tiger beneath her feet. *Jai Mata Di.*

Modesty bears its costs, and the cost for an Indian woman is her dignity.

Her dignity when she is forced to serve tea to strangers who intend to bed her one night after seeing her feet. Her dignity when she is stopped from going to school for the sake of her brothers and is instead hidden behind the walls of a hut in the middle of a city. Her dignity when men talk about her body, brazenly, in front of everyone to see. Her dignity when he prescribes discipline for her newfound feminism. Her dignity when she is violated in a locked bathroom. Her dignity when she participates in consensual, premarital sex.

For an Indian woman faces the consequences of living freely: death.

Her dignity when she becomes her child's mother and her husband's wife. Her dignity when she is hit in front of the family, when she is supposed to abet the violence in silence. Her dignity is her inability to choose any occupation, finding one that doesn't make her feel uneasy. Late night walks and early morning runs are forbidden, as her dignity may not be able to handle the indecision of moving past a group of men as they laugh and leer, or taking the darker road home.

Her dignity is calling a friend at a gas station, afraid that something bad may happen so late at night, six-thirty.

Her dignity is a mutilated body lying in the middle of the streets. Urging pedestrians to focus their pupils on her dying corpse. Beckoning more men to step around her politely instead of brushing up behind her with their cocks.

An Indian woman's dignity is locked within her soul, so that once she does reach heaven, even God will not let it go. For her dignity resides within the Mother, and who isn't as dignified if not the Creator of all mankind?

XXXIII

UNSETTLED

——

WASHINGTON, 14 MAY 2020

All morning, I felt unsettled by the fact that Omar's Indian. I didn't like it. In the grain of my being, I've realized I can't trust men from my country. Not with this, not with sex. They've been taught, no, trained, to believe a woman's body is not her own. Most of them anyway. We don't talk about sex in South Asian households. We don't talk about sex as pleasure, in any case. All my grandparents want are great-grandchildren to play with. Sex for procreation, not pleasure, not love, not fun.

I felt unsettled because in a heartbeat, Omar could completely shatter my reality. I sent him too much of my body—my face and everything else—and even I know that. What I forgot were my boundaries. The audience rarely sees the behind the scenes. There always is the arm's length, the curtain call, backstage, end of a show to fall back on. He didn't ask for that much more, but I was readily available. Boredom pulls the knobs out of my system and cranks my senses way down. Boredom wants me to seek adrenaline and pain, thrill, and excitement. A never before seen trick. Boredom feeds on my need for distractions. The boredom when Ben is gone.

I felt uneasy the entire day. I wanted Omar to stop messaging me out of his own boredom, I didn't want to keep stringing him along in a way. But, I couldn't just stop it. I couldn't do anything if his boredom got the better of me and released my hidden self to the world.

I wanted to puke. My heart was constricting, and I gagged at the thought of him saving my pictures. He was too close to home, barely a few minutes away by car. *I mean, I could even walk down the bridge and get to U-District.* Not thousands of miles away like Ben. I cared that Omar was almost next to me; so close I could hear his breathing, and his whispers. So close I could almost feel his hands on my skin.

I felt skin. My skin, between my fingers, almost like I was seeing myself as an outsider. I didn't want to be touched. Even as my nerves prickled while I tried to comfort myself, rubbing my thighs and arms to comically warm myself up. As some unknown alter ego, *another* Nat. I felt shame. Bile rose up, and I forced myself to gulp in a few breaths of air to suppress my nausea. I felt… stupid and foolish and completely irresponsible and idiotic and self-victimizing. This was what being an adult was about, right? A notional consent. *Can someone withdraw consent after the act? Am I safe by just blocking him and forgetting about last night? Will he be angry that I blocked him? Is it my safety or his? Should I delete the app and reinstall it, so all the conversations delete (at least on my mind)? Out of sight, out of mind. Does anyone have to actually listen to you weep?* I felt… used. Insanely, utterly used. And not in a good way, making me breakfast in bed after a long-night kind of way. A panicked, stomach-churning used.

A few more breaths in.

A few sips of water later.

I still felt deplorably used.

Used for pictures and some one-time fling. But also, used for being desi, almost like he had that power over me. I barely even knew Omar, but he felt way more tangible than Ben. I'm so scared my first time will be a violation of my trust, nothing but a one-night rush. I don't want to feel unsettled, or used, or scared.

I'm scared.

XXXIV

NOT REALLY INDIAN

Ever since she had moved to the US, Nat could feel it in her bones. An urgency to return to her homeland, the motherland, her birthplace, her family. A fever that extended into every decision, every small choice she made, separated by the seas and the continents. Steps and choices that would lead her farther and farther away from her *desh*, her land, India.

She missed it. The pollution, the politics, the festivals, her grandparents, her cousins, the languages, the brightness. For in the US, everything always looked so dull. The air would smell crisper, sure, but the gray and black monochrome glazed over any appearance of yellow, shining sunlight. In India, everything seemed to be spotlighted by the vibrant saffron, the indigo, the green. The noise accentuated the visuals, the constant honking of car horns and yelling of pedestrians and stall owners. The pungent aromas, everything from jasmine flowers to the auspicious marigold to the scent of *mehendi* to cow manure. The stocky, concrete buildings coupled with the sprawling office parks with skyscrapers and sparse greenery. The flyovers, supported by tremendous pillars, that seemed a little too comfortable to be so high in the sky. The swarm of people, crowding onto the streets and the footpaths, pushing and pulling like a sea of tightly packed sardines. Nat admitted this was an unfortunate romanticization of an unceremoniously backward country. India was moving, yes, but slowly and in a diagonal. The population rapidly increases as does the dispensation of mobile phones and LED screens. A country of haves and have-nots.

Her homeland.

Nat would never be able to extricate herself from its grasps, its strong spindly arms and curious tail. India was her Hanuman, carrying her thousands of miles from her home to where she was destined: America. India was a feeling and a memory. India was love and hate. She had lived the highest highs of her childhood in India. She had seen her first globe in India, dug her toes into the warm Indian Ocean, felt the pangs of a puppy love (not the jacked up, intense, hormonal shit she felt for Ben), spent hours puzzling over which books to buy. She had taken long, winding bus rides with the salty wind spraying over her face and hair. She had made her first friends in India. And that would always define her.

As would growing up as a teenager in an insular upper-upper-middle-class neighborhood in Washington State, five minutes away from Bill Gates. Walk two streets, and she could see the Puget Sound, stretched out, proud, imposingly breathtaking. Walk two streets in the opposite direction, and she could see the snow-capped, towering Cascades. She could cover Mount Rainier with her thumb and forget about the mountains for days, but even she grudgingly acknowledged the magnificence of such natural beauty. The bluest of waters, greyest of skies, chilliest of days, all in Washington. While she was just born in India, she was made in America and that hurt her. It tore at her identity, her self-determination.

She didn't know how much to compensate for her American-ness in India, and her Indian-ness in America. The chasm spanned nine thousand miles, and the thousands of ancestors she had left behind.

The New World and all its flaws appealed to her sensibilities as an adult. She liked pothole-less highways, and fast-food restaurants dotting its exits. She liked the overt polity, the Americana, the kindness of her neighbors. She liked its laws and the way of its land. She liked that American trials are speedier than Indian ones. And that one actually could memorize the US Constitution. She knew, deeply, profoundly, she would never be able to identify as just Indian again. She didn't like the pollution or the traffic or the honking that never seemed to end. She didn't like the dust or the lizards. She didn't like the spitting, the pissing, the shitting. She didn't like the obvious class divides, yet she knew she couldn't bear to be without it. She was, almost assuredly, South Asian American or desi American, or if it came to hyphenation, Indian-American. She was not an NRI—a non-resident Indian. She was way, way past that.

She felt a pang of loss when carrying her new blue passport, emblazoned with the United States seal, as opposed to her old blue passport, embossed with the Ashoka Pillar. The foreignness of living in India. The differences in workplace culture. The differences in dating; in love. For nineteen years of her life, she had lived as an Indian citizen. For nineteen years, she had prescribed to an old-school immigrant story, concluding with the prized American citizenship.

She grew up.

Quickly.

Unnecessarily.

Forcibly.

And, for her, growing up meant forgoing part of an ingrained identity with another.

Nat could close her eyes and watch scenes from her life as though in a cinema hall. Swimming in the apartment pool, bubbles popping at the surface as she sputtered, nearly drowning. Loud Diwali crackers being set off way past midnight. Sleepy trips from the car to her bed, being carried by her mum or dad, with bleary-eyed awareness and a tight fist around her parent's neck. Sitting on the shoulders of her relatives, looking past the crowds and onto the ocean. The auto rides home, smoke and dust whipping through her hair, the cigarette scent that would glaze her mum's *dupatta*. Scenes she had only lived in India, a knot in her throat tightening until she felt her heart bobbing to the top of her palate. She closed her eyes and imagined a different life, one without Lady Liberty, and bore the guilt of leaving. She tasted her childhood, its road-trips, the sand in her hair, bike rides under a tree-canopy. She remembered the thousands, no, tens of thousands, of hugs and kisses, smiles and laughs, and basked in its memory.

India was in her birthright. The anthem still on her lips. The accent still on her tongue. The vaccine scar still on her skin. The people still on her mind. As far as she could get away, India was always going to be with her.

XXXV

OMAR

—

"Hey… Is this Natasha? I'm Omar."

Nat's stomach dropped. She had expected her food delivery person on the other end of the line, *not* the guy she had accidentally given her number to three days ago. She had even rehearsed the little 'that's alright' and 'thank you,' at the end of the call when the food delivery person would inevitably tell her the restaurant was out of fortune cookies (she had asked for extra).

"Hey," Nat's voice rose in pitch slightly, and she quickly exited the living room, shrugging at her confused mum and mouthing, "Delivery." Nat made her way back to the bedroom feeling anxiety rush over her. "I—I didn't think you saved my number." She sat cross-legged on her bed and leaned her head on the wall. Her heart was thudding against her chest.

She heard him snigger over the phone and she scowled, setting her jaw in place. "Is that accent real?" Omar teased, almost innocently.

Nat bit her tongue. "Yes. Yeah, it is. Unfortunately." Scowling, she still held the phone close to her ear, bristling at his offhanded question.

"Hm…" Omar paused, and she could hear him swallow and take a breath in. "Um…"

"Why did you call me," Nat sighed, "Omar…?" She hesitated at his name, taking a silent breath of air in and putting the phone in speaker.

His voice crackled through. "I—I didn't think you were real."

"Well, I am." Nat chewed the inside of her cheek. "Do you mind if we switch to text? I—"

"Why?!" His voice leapt in volume, and she grimaced. "You have such a sweet voice."

Feeling her cheeks flush, Nat slunk under her covers, clutching her phone close to her face. "Why are you calling me, Omar? It's almost one." She spoke gently, frowning.

"Like I said, to check if you were real!" His words slurred slightly at the end, and Nat winced. *He's drunk, the absolute turd.* "And, since you are, and since I am, too—"

"Omar. Let's just talk tomorrow, okay? When you're a bit more sober."

"I am sober!"

"Right." Nat sighed inwardly and looked at the time again. 12:54 a.m. "Okay, then. I'm real, so now what?"

"Hm… I forgot." Omar hiccupped, and Nat swore she could hear someone else over the phone. The beat passed. "Actually, no. I remember now, *yaar*, I was thinking of the pictures you sent me last time."

Nat wracked her memory for that night. *It's been… three days, at least? Which means… Fuck, I don't remember at all.* Opening up **The Chatroom**, she scrolled past the unread messages and into the older ones. *What was his username, again?* "Right. The photo I sent you."

"Nope." Omar drew out the word, slipping to his next thought with drunken haste. "Pictures. You sent me so many pictures."

Right! PicsForChicks—that's his username. Oh, lord, what did I do? Nat assessed the damage: a few random, PG-13 selfies, and at least three off-the-cuff impromptu nudes. *I'm so done with myself. I can't even—*

"Did you hear me?" Omar shouted through the speaker.

"Yes," Nat cleared her throat. "Yep, I can hear you. So, what about those pictures?"

"I want to meet you, *ya*. Is Natasha your real name?"

"You're asking too many questions."

"Sorry," Omar let out a short laugh, and she heard him gulp. "Well, if Natasha is your real name, and you are a real *ladki*, will you show me around Seattle?"

"What?!" Nat rapidly scrolled through their messages, trying to find anything to do with touring the city with this dude.

"You know, like you promised?"

"Look, Omar," Nat started, wincing. "You seem like an okay guy and everything, but I'm not really—"

"It's not a date, dumbo." Omar snapped, before sighing and continuing begrudgingly. "Listen, *yaar*, I haven't really seen the city since moving here, and like I said, I have no friends. So?"

"So, what?"

"Will you show me around?" Nat could sense his nervousness through her phone. She smiled a little bit in pity.

"Listen, dude. Omar—" she started.

"Don't say no, *yaar*," he said softly with a sigh. "I'm not as much of a *harami* as you think I am. I swear, it'll be a no strings attached dat—meeting, meet-up. Friend date. Hangout.”

“I really can’t… It’s not like everyone’s going out again.” Nat pursed her lips. “Dude, I don’t even know who you are.”

“How can you without meeting me?!” Omar retorted indignantly. “One meeting. Someplace safe, not so crowded, and outside so masks would be optional. One time and I won’t bother you again.”

Nat chewed at the inside of her cheek. “I’ll…”

“Please don’t say no, *yaar.*”

“I’ll let you know, ok?” Nat sighed inwardly. “Soon-ish. I don’t want to lie to my parents.”

“Dude, it’s not like we’re going to be doing anything.”

“Right.” Nat rolled her eyes and had the sudden urge to chuck her phone across the room—or end the call before she agreed to something she wasn’t sure she wanted to do.

A moment passed, and she could hear his breath then a gulp.

“So…” Omar cleared his throat, and she heard him shift as a loud rustle crackled through the speaker. “You’re Indian?”

“*South* Indian.”

“Huh. I don’t really like South Indians.”

XXXVI

DAKSHINA

———

I'll easily admit that Tamil songs are probably the most beautiful Indian songs. Tamil sounds so good, so syllabic, in melody. Hindi slurs and rhymes the same words together; Urdu has *shayari*; Tamil has Dravid. Urdu has the North, the *Uttar*, and Tamil has the South, *Dakshina*.

Actually, any South Indian love song is a gorgeous tribute to traditional Carnatic music. While the Hindustani speakers of the North have *qawwali* and *mujra* and *ghazals*, there is a special place in my heart for the Trinity, the *veena*, the *mridangam*, and the poetry of *Bharatanatyam*. And our national treasure, A.R. Rahman, who even after three decades copies his own musical motifs while spouting some of the most melodious original pieces. The strings in "Vinnathandi Varuvaayaa" that mimic a gentle breeze, *thendral*, in the background, the lone *shenai* in "Yeh Jo Des Hai Tera," the agony in his own singing voice in "Kun Faya Kun." There's an innocence in his music that has yet to escape him, even after marriage and children and money.

Banana-leaf-scented freshly steamed *idlis* with a little *thuppa*, gunpowder *mulga podi*, some *yenne*. The sizzle of *dosa* batter as it hits the red-hot skillet; the ensuing rush to form a beautifully round spiral, and more *yenne* to crisp up the outer edges. Stuffed *vankaaya*, so tender yet compact, it takes barely a few pinches to mix it with the rice, *anna*. *Thayir sadam*, curd rice, with what we fondly call *kattum-kuttum* in our miniature nuclear family. Mouth-watering, imported *aavakaaya* that flies all the way from my *Ajji*'s kitchen in my dad's suitcase, wrapped in newspaper and in three Ziplock bags. My *Ammama*'s *Mysore paak* and *barfi* that traveled three houses and nine-thousand miles before reaching my college dorm room. The *murukku* my mother saved for me during spring break, the *aloo* fry that never made it past the TSA.

My *Doctor-thatha* and *Ajji*, my *Ammama* and my *Major-thatha*. Their multilingual swirl of politics, current events, and memories. In English, Telugu, Kannada, sometimes Tamil, sometimes Mizo, sometimes Malayalam, sometimes just gestures. Sometimes repeated thrice. Sometimes with a full plate of food in front of us, sometimes in front of the TV. A constant drizzle of anecdotal lessons, vague feelings, and poignant nostalgia. My grandfathers, the polyglots. My grandmothers, the quiet decision-makers. My parents, the remnants of their childhoods and their life together.

Dulqueer's dimples, Mahesh's soft-spoken stature, Dhanush's confidence, Prabhudeva's dancing, Suriya's acting chops, Arjun's drunken pain, Fahadh's expressive eyes, Madhavan's smile, Nivin's many faces, Siddharth's smolder, Vijay's intensity, Rana's voice, Prabhas' stunts, Rajni's swagger.

Aishwarya's blue eyes, Kalki's innocence, Deepika's long-limbed confidence, Trisha's likeable girl-next-doorness, Asin's bubbliness, Rekha's agelessness, Vidya's candor, Nithya's confidence, Pallavi's self-assuredness. Samantha's cuteness, Nayanthara's sustained successfulness, Tabu's literal perfection.

My life in the *Dakshina* is an unfinished song, a *raga* that hasn't been blessed by the hands of Thyagaraja. It floats aimlessly in the pits of my brain and around my conscience. My life, here in the US, hasn't had the chance to bloom yet; it's a bud, glistening in the morning dew of my youth and my inexperience. It was planted some ten years ago, in a red house with a cherry tree, a dilapidated half-court, and overgrown bramble. A house with prunes and sour apples, rosemary and mint. A house with its own glass bubble on its exterior, keeping away the spiders and the fallen evergreen needles. A house that creaks and groans under my father's footfalls and my strides. A house that holds everything materially dear to us, that we know. Somewhere so far, and so cold, it bears little resemblance to the place of my birth. Instead, our home is so far removed from our origins that we just miss the *Dakshina*, more.

XXXVII

BREAK KE BAAD

———

CALIFORNIA, 15 OCTOBER 2019

"What are you saying, *beta*?" Her dad's concerned eyes bore back at her from the pixelated, six-inch screen. Her mum was next to Vikram, seated at their dining table. It was an uncomfortable position—they were in portrait mode, and all Nat could see of Geet was some curly hair and a shoulder and an eye peering back at her. Nat swallowed, and blinked slowly. She pressed her chest uncomfortably against the wooden college-requisitioned desk, leaning in. A loud shout from a group of passersby outside her open window interrupted her train of thought. The heater whirred patiently in the background, hopelessly combatting the barrage of cool air from outside.

"One sec, guys. Let me shut the window." Raising from her awkwardly low chair, Nat turned to the window and started opening the blinds to shut the window. Making, and then hastily withdrawing, eye-contact with a random passing student, Nat hurried to shut the window. The noises from the bustling evening campus were sucked out of the room like a vacuum. The heater purred, and she could hear her dorm mates down the hall erupt in laughter. Settling back into the chair, Nat moved the phone farther back on her desk, allowing her parents to have a better view of her dingy room.

"Well," she started, waiting as the bandwidth dropped awkwardly and further pixelated her parents' faces. Nat could feel the sting of tears, as she had the sudden realization that she really was alone in California. She could feel the panic in Vikram's voice, the hot tension in the air even though they were hundreds of miles away. "I can't be at school next semester. I think, if I do stay, I will never be the same person again."

She continued, watching their helpless faces blink into high definition for a second before the lag took over. The bland beige and brown hues of their kitchen was only further emphasized by the dingy, sparse yellow lighting in her parents' house. It didn't feel like her home anymore. It was as though a part of the interior, the space that she inhabited, had been carved out when she had left for college.

Nat cleared her throat, "Two nights ago, I was talking to Rumi… And, she caught me in a moment where I was, like, just not present. And, she asked me… 'Are you sure you want to be there?' As in, do I want to be in college?" Trying to gauge their reactions, she paused. There was another unbearable silence from her parents—Vikram looking stonier, and Geet placing a calm, placating hand on his arm. A small gesture in Nat's favor. "I couldn't lie… to her. I said no."

"Daddy, I—"

"Okay, *beta*. It seems you've already made this decision." Vikram's jaw had locked, and he was still. He thought for a second, trying to gather an appropriate response. A fat tear dropped on Nat's hand, all the way on her lap, and then another and another. Suddenly, she was uncontrollably crying.

"I can't cry by myself, so I'm sorry that you have to see me like this—"

"*Beta*, we're your parents. If we can't see you cry, who else can?" Nat could feel the pain in Geet's voice as her mum moved the phone camera towards herself. Geet looked weary, and her eyes sad. "Listen, no matter what, we'll always love you and support your decisions. If you think, this is the best thing to do right now… We'll want you to do it, ok?"

Another beat of stillness, silence, other than the odd sound from her next-door neighbors. A creak or bass line.

"Natasha."

Nat froze mid-flinch, her heart beating rapidly as her father broke the silence. Even at nineteen, hearing her full name brought back memories of time-outs and the occasional spanking. She mustered up the courage to stare back at him from the shelter of her dorm room, hundreds of miles away. Her parents rarely called her by her full name; while both versions were English-compliant, Natasha always felt heftier on accented tongues. More burdensome, with each intoned syllable.

"I—I never thought…" Vikram's voice broke up. She didn't know whether it was from some unknown emotional reaction or her Wi-Fi connection, "…that you would be in this position. If I did, I may have asked you to stay closer to home or to have taken a gap year before going. I'm not going to stop you, *beta*, but your reasons have to be solid. You can't come back home and waste time doing the random crap you and your mother do all night—" He glanced at Geet, who was glaring at him, mouth half-open about to interrupt. "Sorry, sorry."

Vikram cleared his throat and tilted the camera back in his direction. "What are your plans? If you come back home.

How will that interfere with your overall college timeline? Have you spoken to your advisor? Are you prepared to take a semester-loss academically? How will it affect your—" He broke off. Geet had placed another, firmer, hand on his shoulder.

"Tasha-baby, do you want to do this or are you being pressured?"

"Pressured, by who?!" Nat snapped, her brow creasing frustratedly. "Rumi didn't force me to say this, she just helped me come to this conclusion. I can't survive here. I can barely eat anymore. I don't go out. I have zero friends, who'd come and support me. I'm drowning in work. I feel like I've lost the person I was for, like, my entire life. And, I'm not even working out by myself, because I'm shit scared to even enter our gym. Like, I can't go in. Every time, I think about all the girls there who actually know what they're doing and already look amazing."

Nat stopped midway through her rant, and looked back, flushed, at her parents. They stared back in a shocked silence, and her dad was the first to break it.

"Natasha."

She flinched.

"Nat…" Vikram restarted, more gently. "*Beta*, I want you to sleep on it, okay? Just for a night or two, maybe until the weekend? Even better, don't think about it until Thanksgiving. We'll be able to meet and talk and you can figure out if you really want to go for it then… Okay?"

"I'm sorry for getting upset, Dad. Mama. I don't want you guys to think I'm being dramatic or weak. It's literally how I feel right now, and I can't help it. At all. I feel like—"

"*Beta*, sleep on it, okay?" Her dad suddenly looked a thousand times more tired than he had a few moments ago. Nat blinked, and felt herself start crying again. She brushed her tears aside, hastily, as more dripped onto her lap. Vikram sighed, "I don't want you to stress out about us, okay, *beta*? Just… we feel helpless. And, I think if you keep talking it through with us, we might be able to understand."

"I'm sorry, Daddy." Choked up, Nat blurted and cried frustratedly into her hands, trying to make herself stop. "I think I need to hang up so I can wash up…"

"Okay, *beta*," her mum's voice tinkled from the speakers, and Nat smiled weakly. "Call us anytime, yeah?"

"Yeah, Mama." Nat clutched her phone, ready to end their call. "I'm sorry, again, Daddy. I didn't mean to be like this today… Happy birthday, again. Sorry for being a party-pooper."

Ignoring her parents' protests, Nat ended the call, and tossed her phone aside. She moved slowly to her sink and splashed some water over her face. She looked up, on her tip-toes, trying to catch a glimpse of her red-eyes in the too-tall mirror. Nat felt a pang in her chest as she started getting ready for a shower. It was already 10 p.m., but she felt dirty all of a sudden. And tired. So, so exhausted, especially when thinking about the next month-and-a-half before Thanksgiving.

Lip trembling, she locked her dorm door and walked across the hall into the bathroom. For now, at least she had A.R. Rahman to keep her company. And her handy Bluetooth speaker.

XXXVIII

TAILSPIN

———

I have self-induced music flashbacks. Listening to playlists from 2018, I can recreate the exact emotions I dealt with in my senior year of high school. The tragedy of an end, the excitement of new beginnings, the melancholia of leaving a second and first home. "Tailwhip" is that song for me. I mean, all of the singles from the French-Canadian band *Men I Trust*, newest album *Oncle Jazz*. Every one of them, as quickly as they appeared on Spotify, I added them to my playlists and marinated in my fading teenage angst every day after school. Even now, more than two years later, every emotion breathes into life. I watch them streaking across the room like paint and splashing me with some color. Blues and yellows, mostly. Sads, and happys. No anger, surprisingly. In my senior year, I never felt that white-knuckled, blood-boiling rage I used to in other more stressful years. I felt pleasant and at ease. But not numb.

Today, I just feel numb. Recursive in a lot of ways. I keep doing the same mind-numbing and emotion-blurring tasks. Watch TV, eat, sleep, inject myself into my writing. Ponder on my life's trajectory. Shudder at the thought of returning to school. Watch TV, eat, don't sleep. Stay up until dawn listening to Indian love songs and shivering under the bed-sheets with bloodshot eyes.

It's a life. Maybe it's not my own yet. My euphoric episode has lasted its full stay, extended its welcome it thinks. I know it should exist year-round, like Florida tangerines or Japanese apples. Instead, I have it in bouts and spurts. Most of the time, I feel as though a weighted blanket has been pulled over my head. Suffocated and sweaty even in the freezing early spring months.

"Tailwhip" is the song I listened to in college when I was feeling particularly depressed or nostalgic or depressgia. I needed an option that didn't include me crying in an empty room, alone. Listening to my favorite playlist from 2018 did the trick, apparently. I could only microdose "Tailwhip," how-ever. An abuse of good things would only lead to more toxicity. Like coping with the stress of college with movies. Rewatch-ing old ones, watching new ones, gulping them down in six-hour weekday sessions rather than once during the weekend. It almost felt as though the moment I stopped watching, the house of cards I had built around me would come crashing down. I wouldn't have any option but to be exposed. Crying in public places, eating at the dining hall, alone. Smiling at strang-ers, even though it was never reciprocated on campus. A smile that could go so far in high school, seemed to depreciate in value. A smile wasn't even necessary at the campus coffeeshop.

The emotional blockage from college still hasn't drained from my system. My emotional lymphatic nodes have not yet processed the extent of what I felt only a few months ago. I was so depressed; I was so stuck. Immovable, complacent. I haven't dealt with the gravity of the wreckage that still keeps trying to suck me into its orbit. It looms over me some days, and if the day is clear enough, even my parents seem to notice the constant thunderstorm over my head. They don't understand it, and I don't blame them. The quintessential first-world problem: being unhappy at a place of secondary education. Literally every student I've met has had to grapple with leaving home or their friends in some way, yet they got past it. And, from what I could tell, completely past it. So much so I couldn't stand myself while surrounded by them. Those who were past the sadness… the homesickness… the loneliness…

The feelings I tried my best to forget by losing myself in the noise and the symphony of it all.

Another underappreciated musical moment in my personal history is the song "Kun Faya Kun" from A.R. Rahman's *Rockstar* album. Of course, this is more filmi and less obscure when compared to a French-Canadian band with a million monthly listeners on Spotify. *Rockstar* (2011) was a massive hit when it released and everyone lauded Rahman for its soundtrack: "Tum Ho" ("You Are"), "Aur Ho" ("And More"), "Naadan Parindey" ("Innocent Birds") and "Kun Faya Kun." The last song is seven minutes long; the YouTube video is a little shorter and includes dialogue from the film.[5] With my eyes on Ranbir Kapoor for three-sevenths of the time and on my work for the rest, I listened to it on repeat while studying in my college dorm. And dealt with whatever I was feeling in true Sufi-fashion: through *qawwali* and the Qur'an. The phrase "Kun Faya Kun" appears several times in the religious text, and means "be, and it is."[6]

Hence, I was and so it be.

---

5   "Kun Faya Kun Full Video Song Rockstar | Ranbir Kapoor | A.R. Rahman, Javed Ali, Mohit Chauhan," posted on December 5, 2011, YouTube video, 6:20.

6   Sayyid Kamal Faqhih Imani, "Section 14: Surah Al-Baqarah, Verses 116-117," in *An Enlightening Commentary into the Light of the Holy Qur'an vol. 1*, trans. Sayyid Abbas Sadr-'ameli (Imam Ali Foundation), 194.

XXXIX

RUMI

—

To: Rumi

Sun, June 7, 7:19 am

Hey

hey?
why are you up so early

Lmao, I literally could ask you the same thing
Anyways
I had a dream

lolll is that why youre up then?
is it the one i'm thinking about

Um, kinda. I never slept lol
This time
I think I dreamed of Ben too

what the fuck did he do to deserve THAT much love lol

Nothing! -__-
He just idk

bruhhh yuo are ins omuch trouble
youve literarlky fallen in love with his stupid ass

Omfg
NVM THAT
can i tell you abt teh dream

yeah, yeah ok

ok so like
I was in my bedroom, right?
On my bed, just kinda chilling
and then all of a sudden
there are like a
thousand
ants on my body
big ants
little ants
the ones that look like cartoon characters
but also real looking ones

...what the actual fuck Ant
i mean Nat

wait
i've got more
and iw as freaking oout
every second i moved
i could feel them crawling up

and down on my skin
walking around like they
like
owned my body
idk

Nat is there something i should know about?
have you been speaking to your therapist???

shh, yes, besides the point
anyway
so i keep swiping away at them
killing them basically
and i can smell their blood

wait, is that an actual thing?

What??

smelling the ants blood

Yup. :| it's a thing,
it's really fucking weird
and gross, my dude

okie ok go on

so smelling blood
i realize i'm pretty much naked
or at least in that new lingerie
i told you about?

9 dollar panties?

yup
and when i turn on my side
to look at the rest of my bed
i see
him

wait wait wait when did Ben send face pics????

never.
i
i just see his hair and like a body
but i fucking swear to you
it was him

and???
what??

the ants were gone.
like that they just
disappeared
and i reached out to that side
and it felt like it was taking forever
for me to put a hand on him

bish wtf

and i woke up

...

seriously are oyou ok?

Yes!!!
Ig this time was super diff
from my last few dreams

uh no shit
this has some type of universe sign shit all over it
what did your OCstar say today?

Wym?

i mean.

oh "you have the power
to be the change
you want to see"

you were talking to like
wtf does that even mean loll
30 different guys online

Hahahaha, yeah this one was kinda bs???
Sure, but that was only like for a few days
And tbf it was def more in hundreds :|

and??? then ben shows up and suddenly
all your attention is on him
you haven't even told me about that guy you met

Omar? Oh yeah!
We had our second date last night
I snuck in, that's why I'm up early lol
Uh, I am officially not a virgin anymore

WHAGTTTHEfuck
omg you didn't even tell me

                              tbh, i kinda forgot.
                              he was... disappointing

lolllll
i told you
its kinda overrated and
you like ben too much, Nat

                    Rumi, don't pull that shit dude
                    i've wanted to lose it forvere
                Omar is sweet too and he's desi...
                    ok, jk that really creeps me out
                          but he has a penis so

omgomg so it was okay?
like was it good or horrible??

                              I'll tell you later!
                          Let me finish the dream!

what
i thought it wa sover

                              I just remembered
                      When I was super into Ryan
                I used to have a really similar dream
            Except I was in the bullpen of my old school
                  and i was watching him play baseball
                          or run or something

                                    and I felt like an ant on my arm
                                    And he turned and smiled at me
                                        and the ant vanished

hm
what's with you and ants

                              BUT THOUSAND MORE APPEAR
                              idk dude i think i'm terrified of them
                                    but when they're around

wait what how many????

                                        i find it super easy to just
                                                kill them
                                    that sounds so fucking dark
                                          ahahahahahaha
                                    like at least thirty or forty idk
                              but i've had another version of the dream

ok.............

                                    where if he doesn't smile
                                          or i ignore him
                                    the ant just disappears or
                                       i swipe it away and kill it
                              the less attention the better i guess

Natasha
sometimes you can really
freak me out

Same to you buddy <33

oml stop

Wait, can you video call?
I coulda probs told you all this in a call lol

not right now
you caught me on
my ten minute poop break

O.o wow
just. Just call me later

ughh you're so lame

From: Rumi

Mon, June 8, 10:53 am

ik its before noon and youre probs sleeping
but i was in zoology and
i was thinkng about what u said earlire
whatif the guys in your life are like ants
like each one of them ca n carry a lot of weight in your life
bc yk ants are super strong
or at least they used to
and any little bit of attraction youd give is
liek your sugar???
so you accidentally spill sugar aka give HIM attention
and suddenly
the whole colony has moved in

and now u have an ant problem
and while its easy to get rid of with insect killer or whatever
youre using some wack organic shit that doesn't work that well
so you still have that ant problem
but it's always easiest to just… ignore
and then they go away and tada
and
ok idk where i'm going with tihs

To: Rumi

Mon, June 8, 12:38 pm

lmao what the hell
ok ms. freud
"interpretation of dreams" kinda day lol

12:40 pm **Rejected Call**

bish what are you doin rn

bruhh
im in class gtfo

okie okie sorry

Tue, June 9, 3:04 am

dude
i remember why i'm scared of ants
i was fting my cousin
and she reminded me of how we like
tried to attack a red anthill once

and it backfired and the entire
house went from 0 to 100 real quick
and we had like a thousand ants
inside the kitchen
and my entire foeram was covered in bites
up to my elbow because i was trying to get rid of
an entire cake in the pantry

fuck
i still have the scar on my pinky
how tf did i forget that????
Also, I really liked the point you made
I think in some wyas my subconscious is
just telling me to chill tf uout
around all these dudes
or at least that
ultimately
i have the final say to end things
with them or within myself

i've been speaking to Omar more
i kinda like him now :3
okay he still is super weird and
really awk in general
ughh
he basically said point blank that
his parents wanted him to marry someone
muslim lmao and north indian
so wtf is up with that?!
idfk
lmao i would say sry for t eh text dump
but yk me too well bby

XL

LOVE

——

"You better not fall in love with me," she teased from the doorway, a toothbrush dangling between her lips. While she was acutely aware of her big, bulging stomach and the fat rolls on her back, Nat never minded looking her most run down in front of Omar. She threw him a kiss, and turned back to face the mirror, certain he was appreciating the view.

"You don't have to worry about that."

Nat heard the rustling of the sheets as he got up and approached her from the back. Omar planted his chin on her shoulder, and teasingly blew into her ear. Squirming away, she spit into the sink and watched as he got into the shower. The curtains scraped against the rod, and the torrent of water started. "When are you going back?"

"Come in and find out."

Rolling her eyes, she finished brushing and stuck her hand into the shower, expecting to surprise him. Instead, he pulled her in, drenching her with the water. "Shit, Om. You didn't have to do that!" Scowling, Nat ran her hands through her now-wet hair and looked up at him blankly. "So… when?"

"Next month. I think during the long weekend for Fourth of July. Tickets were super cheap," he shrugged nonchalantly and grabbed the shampoo. The shower was starting to get hotter, and steam escaped from the top. Nat could feel beads of sweat appearing on her body, and she shoved in front of him to start washing herself. "You know, mummy-papa found eight girls for me. One by one, we'll see them all. Fuck, *yaar*, they want me to get married by next month…"

She smirked while lathering her scalp and turned to face him. "*Accha hi hai.* As soon as you go back, *shaadi kar ke* fuck some random girl, *na*?" He frowned and stopped rinsing off. Suds fell to his shoulder, and she playfully swatted them away. "Just joking, *ya*. It's good! You'll at least have the chance to properly be with someone."

She watched as his Adam's apple bobbed and looked up at his eyes. Omar stood still for a few more seconds before leaning in and kissing her deeply. She felt the tiles on her back as he moved closer, his arms around her now.

"*Arrey, yaar,*" he pulled back and took a long pause. "You've killed my mood again."

"Doesn't *look* like it, *haan*, Omar?" She laughed and groaned after a pang of betrayal showed on his face. "Okay, okay, *baba*. I won't say anything about your impending wedding and *baraati*. By the way, are any of the girls hotter than me? I kinda want to see some pics, now. Hell, are *you* even allowed to see pictures of them? Being Muslim and all."

"*Kyun*? Why do you care?" A sly grin appeared as he rubbed her head violently in an attempt to rinse her hair. "And, yes, I have seen their pictures, thank you very much. My parents aren't that old-fashioned."

"Ow, fuck, *behenchod*. Why would you do that?!" Nat fumed, and started applying conditioner. "Oh, definitely, just old-fashioned enough to get you married to another Qureshi?"

"Listen… Whatever happens, I'm always here for you," he said in a low voice, sincerity smeared all over his face. "You know that right?"

"What *bull*shit. *Dekh*, I like you, Omar. But, we both know just how much we were never supposed to be a thing. I know you think I want a relationship—I don't." She stopped to gauge his reaction, continuing slowly. "I also want the best for you, which means, after—I guess, next month—we won't ever see each other again." She cupped his cheek, trying to memorize the feeling of his beard and jaw.

Omar nodded thoughtfully, his fingers playing with her hair and absentmindedly brushing the side of her chest. Again, he leaned in to kiss her. This time, she pushed him to the other wall, pressed up against his body. They remained silent for the rest of the shower, taking their time and slowly coming to terms with the end of their time together.

When they finally exited their shower together, the sun had just started dipping under the horizon. Nat wrapped herself in the towel she had brought and tiptoed around the room barefoot before pulling on some socks. "Hey, you should show your new wife that thing I taught you… Guaranteed first-class first time." She winked and guffawed stupidly. "And, don't be an asshole, ok? Remember that women are people, too…" Rolling her eyes, Nat stood up and turned towards Omar, pulling off her towel in a grand gesture and plonking it onto her head. She shook her hair, watching his reaction as the water spun across the room and onto him. "*Chal,* I'll treat you to dinner before you leave, okay? I can make my famous desi-ish pasta thing."

Omar observed her with a half-smile, and he proceeded to dry off awkwardly near the door. "What trick, *baba*?"

Natasha didn't want it to end. Not because Omar was an outstanding lover, or really that intelligent. She just enjoyed his company even with his eccentricities and occasional abrasiveness. His presence was enough to ease those long nights and cold mornings. He wasn't too old, and he wasn't exploiting her; it was a mutual agreement. She was using him as much as he was using her. He swore he didn't know her dad, and she forced him to delete all the pictures he had sent. Not that it did any much to calm her anxiety. They were still sneaking around in the middle of a pandemic. Nevertheless, she liked his newfound adulthood, his independence from parents or heritage. She appreciated that he didn't expect anything more than what she was willing to give. And, he didn't lie. Well, at least, not too much.

The first time they met, it was at a cute outdoor cafe that Nat had suggested. She was seated at a small table, ten minutes early, and gulping down an entire glass of water, attempting to quell her nervousness. Her eyes were fixated on the entrance of the restaurant, chewing at her lip and constantly tying and retying her hair. Finally, with her hair down, he arrived at the entrance and Nat sheepishly waved him over. He made a vague comment about the choice of cafe, and tapped the table impatiently, flagging down the waiter. *How anticlimactic,* Nat sucked her teeth in annoyance.

Omar incessantly made fun of her height—sometimes weight, sometimes language—and acted the role of a friend, rather than a lover. He prodded at her weight and she had lost her appetite quickly. Omar laughed with his mouth wide-open, and sometimes with half-chewed food in his mouth, too. Nat had grimaced and bit her tongue. Even with all his unappetizing behaviors, the conversation had flowed smoothly from his upcoming graduation to his dream job to parental expectations. Omar was nearly done with his master's degree in... some form of engineering or another. He was twenty-six and was just starting his life. In a way. He was still answerable to his parents' desires and impromptu video calls. She found herself laughing with his stupid slack-jawed chortle, and even suggested a gelato spot nearby. Even after noticing how he stared at the rivulets of water dripping down her shirt when she accidentally spilled her drink. He had been quick to hand her a napkin and shift his eyes to her face even if just for the briefest minute before his gaze moved to her chest again.

It was only during their second meeting, when he had shut the door to his studio behind him, Omar made her feel like a queen. He took his time, and she was able to see him in a different light. He moved slowly and carefully, as though opening a long-awaited present. In some ways, that was exactly what she was. His much-anticipated gift. With that second meeting, she no longer felt like she had the same body. The sex wasn't very good, and he definitely finished too quickly, but she had expected that. After all, it was her first time and she hadn't expected too much at all. Laying on her back, and finally noticing some of Omar's oddities, she then initiated the second and third rounds.

She felt at an ease with him. He could understand her Indian-ness. But, he would always undermine her true love affair with her birth country. He didn't really think she would ever realistically return to India. *He wasn't wrong,* she remarked. *But he was an inconsiderate ass, nonetheless.* Omar spent hours reminiscing about Bombay, his house, his school, his favorite *vada-pav* stall. And, she'd listen intently, watching his expressions change and bounce, his hands gesticulating. He wouldn't really hear what she had to say, and she didn't mind. Nat understood that their relationship was temporary, *time-pass* as an Indian would say. His black hair would remind her of Ben and throw her into another tailspin. She'd think about how Ben's lips had felt on her in her dreams, how his mouth playfully swallowed her cold fingers jokingly, and how she would clutch on his curly black hair. Ben was not real in the way Omar, who was snoring lightly by now, is.

PART V

RESIDUE

XLI

WYD

———

12:30ᴀᴍ, 5/23/2020
tanning.chatum is online
brattypatty is online

tanning.chatum is typing...
heyyy

brattypatty is typing...
Hey, B :)

wydd

Nm, jc wbu

lol same playing minecraft

Lmao ok

sorry I've been super busy with school
i miss talking to u tho bitch

Yeah no worries...
lol imy too >.<

tonite we boutta get real wild
its friday night bb

Oh, really?
How wild...?

idk yet but your gonna have to take it

Hahahaha... who says I don't want it? ;P

Stfu bitch

Lol, so hmu later when you're less busyyy
I don't wanna distract you by telling you that I'm about to
go shower lol ;p

fuccc k.
seriously, tonight
i will fuck you

Oh, yeah? I fucking dare you to come and get it ¯_(ツ)_/¯

don't fucking make me bitchhh
k, later then yeah???

aight ;)

12:03ᴀᴍ, 5/24/2020
tanning.chatum is online

tanning.chatum is typing...
hey
i miss you bitch
wyddd

XLII

ANNIVERSARY

———

WASHINGTON, 24 MAY 2020

It's been a hundred days since she had met him. Almost four months since they had started chatting, and laughing, and texting. Four months since she had casually reached out to someone who was just as lonely as she was on Valentine's Day. In four months, she had shed all her online inhibitions, broken a dozen of her well-intentioned rules, and gotten off to a real person, not just online simulacra. Sent him faceless, breastful pictures from her childhood bedroom. Four months since she had thought of him every night. Since she had started imagining his hands on her body, or hearing his quickened breathing next to her ear, or feeling his warmth pressed to her back. Imagining and fantasizing a state of domesticated bliss with Ben, that she had experienced only a little bit with Omar. Going on gelato dates, watching the sunset, cooking for him. Unrealistic and ill-fortuned fantasies about a man, a boy, she'd never meet. Four months since she had listened to music until dawn, thinking of the things she wanted to do with (and to) him. The small gestures she'd introduce to him, her snort, her nervous sweats.

She thought of Ben fondly now, rather than with the same passion she had felt in March. He was part of her life in a small yet significant way and would be a good memory from her youth. Someone she enjoyed, rather than exploited for her own validation. Someone she could fixate her lust onto, an empty vessel, a carrier of sorts. He embodied her ideal man, three thousand miles away. His own shyness now amused her, rather than enticed. She felt her love for him changing, maturing and developing into a place in her heart. Not deep within her belly, not the fire in her stomach, nor the butterflies flying haphazardly through her body. He became a permanent fixture. A friend of sorts. *Will I be able to have a relationship with him* and *with someone in real life?* She mused pensively, late into one of these never-ending nights. The fan was whirring in the background, and a singular lamp cast her entire room in a warm yellow tone. Her hair was still damp from her shower, and she was buried in her Harry Potter sheets, yet again. Her speaker was by her head, and she was listening to The Weeknd's *After Hours* for the third time in the night. She had been scrolling through couple TikTok when she had drawn in a large breath of air and sighed. *Maybe not.*

It was a pity. She wanted to stay in touch with Ben regardless of whether they found someone who could actually inhabit their physical spaces in the future. Someone who could actually touch, kiss, love them. Saddened at the prospect, she found herself experiencing a quaint melancholia. One similar to when she lost her first love. Or, to put it more bluntly, when her first love left her stranded, without closure, ripping at the seams of her heart. Ryan had shattered her heart; Ben, this mysterious more-than-friend, had instead reinstilled her confidence, her sexiness. She became bolder with more people and felt less exposed, even while exposing herself. She felt like an open book, secret-less, anonymous, sensuous. Omar had benefitted the most from her newfound boldness so far.

She wanted to entice more men and, more than anything, exploit this newly installed superpower as an available, and articulate, woman on the internet. While she gave effortlessly, she longed to feel more when receiving. She didn't care if they sent her things to taunt or tease; she just cared whether they thought of her before reaching their climaxes. She wanted to feel good, proud, about that. She merely enjoyed the pleasure they derived from her body. It was new. Effective and efficient. She toyed with the algorithm before settling on the most tantalizing sequence of actions for her to perform. That was what sexting really was at the end of the day: a performance. The long buildup, the extended conversations, the winks, the flirtation before the deluge of pictures and dirty talk.

Like all those strangers online who would disappear after a few hours, in less than four months all her lust for Ben had dissipated. Vanished into thin air or suppressed by her memory. Nat felt jaded. She felt like a scientist, dissecting the ids of dozens of men, getting under the scaffolds of their brains and poking at the most important, primal regions. She wanted a reaction, a response, measurable and confusing. She wanted to understand how she would feel knowing they liked what they were seeing. Whether her cabin-fever would dissipate any feelings for meeting people in real life. Whether her fucked fantasy would exist at the end of this journey. Whether a man at Whole Foods would ask her out to dinner. Whether *this* man at Whole Foods would ask her out.

Or whether she would brood until she stopped feeling anything, before a tsunami of emotions struck her down when she was finally able to return to college. Abrupt, painful, and painfully necessary.

XLIII

19/12/19

———

FLIGHT FROM LOS ANGELES TO WASHINGTON (VIA INDIA), 19 DECEMBER 2019

For some reason, this feels tougher than it did a year ago.

I'm going home.

Even if I have to spend a month in India first, celebrating another Christmas and New Year's Eve away from Washington.

I'll be home in the new decade.

I don't know why my dad agreed to this college break. It really makes no sense, considering I never even told him about the anxiety, the depression, the mood swings, and binge-eating. And, the friendless-ness. This isn't a break to find myself, as much as it is a break to fix what… something… someone has broken. I can't blame every single problem I have now on Ryan, but I can blame myself. It's so easy to forget my naivety and my age. It's so easy to forget the real motivation behind… joining band or the weird summer soccer camp or the even weirder summer science camp. The motivation behind every choice I've made: a boy.

Maybe not "Ryan the First Love" but… I dunno, like, every other guy I've ever liked?!

I shouldn't despise myself for it right? I know I deserve some of the blame, but resentment stinks of future bitterness and self-loathing.

In any case, here I am: whizzing by in another metal tube, with two-hundred odd people, none of them familiar to me. I land in Bangalore in five hours, even though I've been traveling with my three massive-sized suitcases for what feels like a week. Every moment felt precarious, like everything was on the verge of collapse—okay, like *I* was on the verge of collapse. I hadn't slept, or showered, or brushed my teeth in a day. And, I was constipated but constantly hungry.

And, I missed beds.

The movers came earlier than I had expected, and as I was pushing my last box onto the truck, I realized something.

When I get back to school, everything will be different.

My perspective, my sense of belonging, my familiarity, my intelligence, my apathy, my restlessness, my fat, my anxiety, my stress.

Some things will just poof away into thin air, never to be seen again, and I'll be happier for it.

But, some things, some people, will always be the same.

I will always find another Ryan to fall in love with, and another one after. It's a vicious, predatory cycle, and I forget sometimes that I am a snake eating its tail, *not* Sisyphus. I won't be rolling a boulder back to the peak of Mount Olympus, just to watch it roll back down.

No, I am the fucking boulder, and this infinite list of Ryans will hold me steady every time I move uphill. And, they're the first ones to fall as I come back down.

Each of my happy episodes, and my depression reruns will repeat, and repeat, and repeat.

Until I end the cycle…

If I end it…

I don't want to go to India.

I don't want to face my family or celebrate the holidays.

I don't want to be myself anymore and realizing that now, five hours from landing, was just the worst goddamn timing.

I don't want this break to be fruitless and dry; I need to harvest something from this seed I planted in October. I want to harvest my health, my wellbeing. A lifestyle whose benefits I may reap, forever and ever, because of when I sowed this seed, this break. This break may change my life, and it may not.

I must be open to both.

I must be open to failure.

I must be open to defeat.

I must be open to love. Whether it's me, or Ryan, or some other guy, I need to want love before I have it. I need to love myself before I have it, clutch it in my bare hands, plucked from the tree itself, a ripe mango to be cherished and savored. The juices running, sticky sweet fingers, gnawing at a fuzzy pit, and sucking the flavor from it. Letting the mango devour me before I devour it. Relishing this long-awaited delicious satiation.

I'm coming home.

Graduated and stamped, I'm on my way back after so, so, so many days. Enough to smile broadly through the Immigration counter, and converse in a light, happy American accent. Enough to be considered wholly American. I feel at peace with this decision.

I'm taking a break. And, I'm taking it for me and on my own terms.

College isn't going anywhere, and neither are my multitude of Ryans. I'll find them again, all clustered together in some random class or at the gym or at the dining hall.

I don't know. But I know that I will when I see them.

It's only been half an hour since I've been writing. It feels like time is going slower than anticipated. I hope that isn't a common theme for 2020. I hope that I can truly help myself at home, that placing my body in a sanctuary, will contribute to my own healing. I want to ease my pain and soothe the burns with a cooling balm. Who knows what that'll be?

Until then, I have four and a half hours to kill before I hail a taxi, another stinking, rancid vehicle, before I reach my Bangalore. The one of my childhood.

XLIV

TRAUMA

—

Trauma is a difficult thing to talk about. Or process. Or heal from. Or even learn from.

Nat's trauma always felt too simplistic—too superficial, too repressed. Sometimes, too over-processed to even call trauma. The difference between canned tuna and fresh tuna fish is quite stark. The same goes for trauma. Real, genuine trauma doesn't drown in old tinny oil, but in a large freshwater lake. It's caught, it's sudden, and it's sometimes too surreal to really comprehend.

Nat didn't want to call her trauma, trauma. Throughout the years, she would call it many names.

The episode.

That dude from that app.

The picture I sent.

That rushed, frantic midnight call.

The accidental video chat.

In my bed.

In my room.

In my house.

Stupid.

But, never would she call it what it truly was: exploitative, inappropriate, predatory, faux peer-pressure, child abuse, cybercrime, sex crime.

She wouldn't call it out as abnormal behavior from a fifty-year-old man. Or the reason she couldn't sleep some nights, having nightmares about ants, cannibals, and rape. Nat knew inherently that something had died in her after that day. After that evening. After those few moments. She would try her best to forget the bile that rose, and the frenzy in which she rushed to the bathroom, puking her guts into her toilet bowl, eyes streaming from the strain of the vomit. Not tears.

Never tears. That asshole wasn't worth them. He was barely even worth her time. Yet, he had taken so much of hers. Enough to make her first real sexual experience with a man, sullied forever.

Sullied, that is, until Ben. Who soothed her fears, ignored her stretchmarks, and still made her eyes stream—this time with real tears of the confusion and panic that set in once she realized that she loved him. That she was in love with him. That after they'd stop talking, she'd still feel empowered enough to send nudes. To meet people in real life. To dance in a club. To live. And Ben wouldn't be able to leave her system as easily as an impromptu vomit session. So, she had a chance of doing all those things. Nat didn't remember a lot from her childhood, or her younger years, but she was scalded by the memory of that day.

First picture. No face. *Send another one, this time with your face in it.*

Second picture. Face.

A moment passed, and she had deleted the app. Deleted him. Deleted that memory, she thought, or at least the feeling. The sinking feeling of ants crawling all over her body as she rushed into the bathroom and vomited and washed her hair languidly in the shower.

He hadn't even complimented her. But, he was technically in possession of child pornography, now. Maybe he was already in possession of it, she just didn't know. Maybe he had done this to hundreds of little girls online, who wanted some attention or some conversation. Maybe he had just pretended. Nat chose to believe that she was the only little girl he was able to seduce. She wanted to believe that her constant vigilance was because of her own intelligence rather than this incident. She wanted to stop feeling as though oil was coating her tongue, nearly suffocating her, slowing her down every day. That feeling was because of him.

I am nineteen, and I still feel grimy. Will this feeling ever leave me?

He was grooming me.

I was fifteen, and he groomed me.

He groomed me.

I was fifteen, and I was groomed.

I was groomed.

XLV

DUST

———

"We aren't the forever deal, are we?"

"What?"

"The forever deal," she repeated, looking over at him, behind the stacks of books and papers on her desk. She pushed aside the tallest one and raised her eyebrows expectedly. "Frank Ocean?"

They were in a tiny, cramped office; it was midday, and the sun was streaming through the windows, casting a yellowish tinge over the already yellowed pages in clumsy stacks. The traffic honked and raged outside: rush hour in Bangalore was no joke. Decades worth of dust surrounded them, in piles, in the corners, on the books. Resorting to handmade masks, they resolved to remain silent as they worked. They didn't *exactly* know what they were looking for. Only just that they'd know once they found it.

"No… Sorry." He shrugged, "What is that… Is it a song reference?" His back was facing her, and all she saw was his shoulders tense the smallest bit. "You do that a lot, you know."

"Uh, yeah." She laughed it off, and weakly smiling at him. "I'm just messing around." She busied herself with the next tallest stack, pulling out sheathes of paper gingerly.

He smiled back, unsure about what to say. "I am sorry, though." He paused his dusting and turned back to back her.

A dust cloud erupted as the stack of papers came falling down. *Fuck*, she swore in her head, glancing helplessly at the documents scattered all over the floor.

"Hm?" She coughed, not realizing he had said something. "What?" Not realizing he had apologized. Maybe a few days too late, but at least it was here now. Out in the open, scattered all over the floor, ignored, like the pieces of paper.

"Nothing."

"Oh. Ok." She mustered a little more enthusiasm while chuckling and went back to sorting the stacks.

Suddenly, she just dropped everything, and turned to face him angrily. A moment passed, and he hadn't noticed she was looking at him.

"Ben. What are we doing here?"

"I don't know, Nat…" His voice faltered as he finally turned around. She was surprised to see his eyes were moist—dust or guilt, she couldn't tell. "This is your fantasy."

"Right…" She drew out the word and locked her jaw with annoyance. "Why the fuck are you here? In India, with me? In some wack-ass desi police station records storage from the 80s? It looks like I'm about to uncover some big power plant fraud by a Bihari politician. And, why are we wearing masks like it's the COVID pandemic?!"

"I still can't tell you."

"I know… I know… Sometimes, I forget that you were never really real. And, all I'll ever have of you are these—"

"Dreams?"

"It's almost like you're in my head."

"What did you mean when you said forever deal?" Ben sounded sincere. Or at least, she wanted him to sound sincere.

"I meant—" She cleared her throat, and slowly sat down on the floor, gesturing for him to follow. The dust clouds followed their every movement with unsurprising accuracy, swirling up and through the air as they planted themselves on the filthy concrete floor. She leant against the desk, cringing at the thought of washing her hair later in the day. Nat could feel the grime rubbing against her hair and on her pants. She added to the dirt by brushing off her hands on her thighs and looking at Ben pointedly.

"This isn't real."

"No."

"And, if this isn't real, does it mean I never felt anything for you?"

Her fake Ben hesitated, almost as if he were contemplating her question even though she knew his exact reply. "No. No, you felt something because those feelings were real. What wasn't, was your perception of me. Like this, this fake image or mirror of me. It doesn't exist except in your head."

She scoffed and rolled her eyes. Drawing a long breath in, Nat released it slowly, feeling her breath upset the dust once again. "What's with the dust then, if this is all in my head?"

"Oh, baby, if you knew," Ben smirked. "Then, I wouldn't be here." He patted the space next to him and signaled her to move with his head. She sniffed amusedly and scooched herself closer to him. Snuggling next to him, she pressed her cheek against his bicep comfortably.

"What am I looking for, Ben?"

"Love."

"Will I ever find it?" She craned to look up at him. "Will I ever find you?"

"Me?" Ben sniggered, "Fuck, no. I've never been here, remember?"

"Right. Let me know when you get here."

"I was never on my way here." He gently pushed her off of his shoulder, and held her in place, boring holes into her eyes. "I'm not your future, Nat."

She frowned, ever so slightly, displaying her disappointment. "I'm not your past, either. I live between the two. In some sort of *Inception*-style limbo. I'll *always* be here for you—" he poked at the air between the two of them, aiming at her heart, "—but don't expect me to be here whenever you need me. I exist but only when it's convenient for your brain. Not your heart. I'm not going to do the same thing Ryan did."

"What…?" Nat felt a surge of panic rush to her throat, forming an underused lump, urging her to cry. "What do you mean?"

"Ryan never left you. He didn't have the decency to let go of you."

"Don't you mean I didn't have the guts to let him go? Like I'm going to let you go?"

"Why didn't you say bye to him?"

The lump was growing tighter, and Nat felt her eyes swell with tears. "What?" she croaked anxiously. "I—"

"Don't lie to yourself, Natasha. You wanted him to say bye to you just as much as you wanted him to like you. You wanted to feel like he respected you, too. But, guess what?"

Nat could barely speak, but she did, "…what?"

"He will never respect you. You were the little girl that stared at him during class, and said dumb things to him during lunch, and ate lame potato bread sandwiches."

She couldn't take it any further. Nat stood up with a rush, and Ben followed with a similar urgency. "Fuck you, Ben. Fuck you for making me feel special, because obviously I'm never meant to feel this way with another guy for sure. Fuck you for ghosting me. Fuck you for never telling me who you really were. Fuck you for using me a little bit every now and then, while I got too attached to you. Fuck you for never being honest. Fuck your stupid-ass excuses. Fuck you for never wanting me."

Ben watched her pitifully. "I'm not Ben, remember?"

"And, fuck me for being so stupid, and gullible, and easy-to-use, and… fuck me for imagining you in my head. For making up dumb fantasies about a life we will never have together."

His eyes tracked Nat as she raged in the small space, which had suddenly started to feel smaller than when they had first entered. Dust appeared out of nowhere, sending her into a massive coughing fit as her airways filled up with small particulates and a musty scent. Nat gasped and felt her cheeks get wet. "Why don't I feel anything real?" The tears were flowing, now, and Nat wrung her hand at him. "Why can't I anymore?"

"Maybe because you're living in your head?"

"I've always lived in my head."

"Not with Ryan. Or—"

"Sh. Okay, I get it. I fell in love and that was enough to make me realize this Leo has a heart. But, what about… what about me? Why can't I be happy with me?"

"You are happy with yourself. But, you hate how others aren't happy with what you've become. And, you've started to resent yourself for it."

"So… what do I do?"

"You'll tell me in any case."

The irony of the situation was starting to fatigue Nat. She sighed and shrugged. "I guess I will. But, only in the right time, yeah?"

"Yup. I can't know before you know."

She nodded and took a deep breath in. The dust had dissipated. The cramped office, suddenly, felt more like a meadow. The traffic had paused as well to take in a breath of air. The papers were shuffled into their correct spots and the room felt immaculate.

The sun still streamed through the windows. But instead of casting a yellow, pollution-ridden light, it was a warm white. A natural light, just as beautiful as golden hour, but calmer, smoother. A light meant to pull the weight off her chest. Nat breathed in again. Ben watched her from her side, hands in his pockets, and with a small smile playing on his lips.

"Ok. I'll know when I know."

"Or, not."

"Why the fuck would you say that?!"

He shrugged, "I don't know. One can never be too sure."

"Arguing with myself isn't the best thing to do right now, right?"

"If you say so."

"You are" —she sputtered— "so fucking infuriating."

"To be honest, though, like wasn't I always?"

"I forgot why I liked you so much…"

"You liked how I made you feel about yourself."

Nat nodded, slowly, with a creeping sense of shame. "That isn't healthy."

"No, it is not." Ben crouched next to her, carefully sitting down. She could see the individual specks of dust coating his sweater. Nat moved to brush him off as he settled into a comfortable position. "It's the same with Omar, too, you know? Except he's going to leave you soon."

"Hm. Am I going to be sad about him leaving?"

"Maybe. You might," Ben leaned in closer so as to whisper a secret in her ear. Nat flushed as he drew near her. "Or he leaves. You don't bat an eye and move one. What do you think about *that*?" Nat noticed a small scar on his jaw, contemplating his words.

"I should be getting better at having my heart broken."

Ben let out a raucous laugh, and pulled away from her, prompting a huff of annoyance from Nat. "Well, being so self-aware isn't helping your cause."

"Am I therapizing myself?" Nat squinted at yellow sunlight streaming from the half-open windows, avoiding Ben's gaze.

"Only a little."

"Stop enabling me then!" Their exchange reached its climax. Nat sighed again, and wrung her hands, frustratedly. "Why *am* I here, Ben?" She turned to Ben.

"Looking for ant-swers, I guess."

"What in the actual—" Nat grit her teeth at Ben and scoffed. "Is that what the ants mean? A typo for answers? Will I find answers in the ants? Are you so fucking insignificant that I can just squash you away?"

"Sorry. You asked, but I can't really answer, though..." Ben shrugged again, and watched her from those blank eyes. "I think it's time you got out of your head."

"Wait, but I have so much to as—"

WASHINGTON, 7 JULY 2020

Nat woke abruptly with a start. Reaching over to her nightstand, she checked her phone for the time. 6:58 a.m. Shit, she had woken up two minutes before her alarm. And, she was so close to finding out why Ben was in her REM cycle. The sun was streaming through the windows, and she rubbed her eyes, trying to digest what she had just felt. She wasn't over Ben; she definitely wasn't over Ryan, and suddenly. she didn't feel like she was even happy with herself. Just surviving, if that.

XLVI

RO(MAN)CE

———

Can love exist without sex? I've always wondered this. Depictions of pretty, pristine puppy love on reels of celluloid. Long walks on white sandy beaches, little asexual touches, deeply gazing into each other's eyes, blushes and butterflies. Is that what love is or are those images just a concentrated essence of romantic *ishq*?

Mohabbatein.

Kaho Na Pyaar Hai.

Amour.

Love.

Is love sending feet pics? Or thinking of them while you brush? Or wanting them to take pictures *of* you? Is it insomnia, late into dawn, listening to love songs? Is it a public proclamation? Is it a public proposal in front of hundreds of people in Disneyland? Is love unconditional? Should it be? Sex, on the other hand, isn't supposed to be publicly displayed. It's lewd and unbecoming of young lovers to grope and make out on the mall escalator or in a parked car. Instead, we just bury teenage sexuality under layers of euphemistic language and chaste depictions of floral conception. Puppy love. Two flowers shaking against each other suggestively, a honeybee buzzing around nearby. Is it time? Does time lead to love? Does love take its own sweet time? And, does love lead to a better time?

Is sex sending feet pics? Or thinking of them in the shower with you? Or about their warm, clothed body pressed against yours? Is it numbness, late into one's twilight years, barely remembering the fumbling in the dark? Is sex always supposed to be good? Can sex be considered a favor for someone else? Or a return gift after an extravagant Valentine's Day dinner? Is sex, ultimately, transactional? Love, on the other hand, isn't supposed to be surreptitiously practiced. It's rude and bizarre for old lovers to bicker and fight in the grocery store or their childrens' houses. Instead, we just bury unromantic love under six feet and silver jubilees. The practicality of procreation and reproduction. Sex is childbirth, and childbirth is progeny. South Asians have practiced this kind of love for generations, a necessary fledgling love that is perpetrated by the parents onto the children. A love that sustains a lineage. Does time kill love? Does love kill time faster? The years keep coming until one day, the love isn't around anymore but you have nowhere else to go. And, no one else to lay next to.

No one has ever looked at me sexually. And I'm not supposed to even feel the slightest bit offended?

No one has held my hand or touched the small of my back. No one has ever wanted me, and I'm supposed to acquiesce to this lack of attention and seduction. No one looks at me twice; I'm supposed to pretend that it doesn't matter? Invisibility isn't so much a cloak as it is a curse. A wrench tightening around my esophagus, a permanent lump in my throat every time I see a couple (real or not).

I feel so deeply I can't see straight anymore. It physically pains me to even think about Ryan for more than a few minutes. What happened to me? What did I do to deserve this stinging numbness? Feelings so blindingly hot, they're almost cold. A numbness to distract, a numbness to stop, a numbness that I just cannot get rid of. How did numbness bequeath me with its presence? What immaculate deed did I do in my twenty years that compels the universe to send me this lump? I'm sick of being a lonely lovesick speck on the face of the Earth.

I want so much that I don't think I'll ever get what I want. Not entirely anyway. How tough is it to ask for someone who… loves me back? Or respects me and knows when to hold me close without being suffocating? I want so much that if I ever do get it, I'd be constantly terrified of losing it all. I don't believe in a love for me. I know, in my heart of hearts and mind of minds, people can never fill the void that *he* left. I wouldn't want to hurt anyone in that way, and *he* had. *He* was the reason for the permanent lump in my throat, and my near-constant moist eyes for almost a decade. Our silver jubilee. *He* was the reason I couldn't watch some movies without imagining our life story instead of the characters.

I'm spoiled by desi movies and the aches in my chest don't help me cope with my feelings. I'm spoiled by the chaste touches, and stolen glances, and the lip-synced lyrics, and the tragedy. Oh, the tragedy of it all. The heartbreak that eventually fades to a "Happy Ever After." And the *saath pheres* around a pyre. I'm afraid to cloud my judgment with other drugs, because love has got me addicted to its lack of feeling in the most insidious of ways. Love motivates me to seek sex in the worst corners of the world, and with questionable characters. Love motivates me to hold my breath in for three hours during an Indian film, and slowly release it as I digest another blistering romance. This time a little less chaste, more depraved, and a little later at night. A lustful love motivates my late-nights and my constant worries.

But even with all this love, all these examples and associations: I don't believe in a love that can coexist within the four walls of my vessel. I believe in concrete floors and a well-broken-in, shingled roof. I don't think I'll ever be held in that *sweet* way or be pulled close to someone or be stared at with an intensity I'm willing to forgive. And, what point does life have without love?

XLVII

S(HE) SAID

———

WASHINGTON 14 JULY 2020 VIRGINIA

NAT   **BEN**

listen
this is how it happened

> she ghosted me for like three days,

i became super busy with work
and just dealing with my own shit

> so i figured

so i figured

> she was off fucking some guy

and we'd talk again
and joke about how work was killing me

and how all i wanted to do
was to… see him or something

i didn't give a fuck, dude
that bitch is out there
and i know she kept talking to random ^*@#^
and sending pics to all of them
i was fucking over it

our six-month talk-versary was coming up
and i was really impressed with us ha
i wanted to do something special
like shave and stuff too

she's some stupid basic bitch
she was fucking like a hundred different ^*@#^

i really thought
one day,

i didn't even ask for shit dude
and she just kept sending the same old

we'd meet
like

ass and tiddies
like she ain't shit,

in real life
and hit it off or at least be
like

fuck man.
i don't even know why
i blocked her

and laugh about the stupid shit
we both pulled
he was busy with school for like the
entire
time

i coulda got more pics
at least
but
fuck
i got super fucking fed up

and, i was gone for
three
days

she fucking left me on read
dude, it's so weird ok
she like confessed and shit or told me some bull about
'having a crush'

i don't know what i did wrong
now, i don't want
to even think about him
when like a week ago
i would have *killed*
to have him in my life

don't worry bout it, man

i really liked him, Rumi

bitches ain't worth shit

i really liked him, Rumi

XLVIII

REINVENTION

In the age of social media and Rupi Kaur's Instagram, how does one reinvent themselves on a public platform?

Will preaching to the body positivity choir do the trick? Or appealing to the masses of queers? Dancing for *America's Got Talent*? How about playing the flute?

How does one reinvent their self?

Is it a lobotomy or liposuction?

A sauce reduction, a red-wine that bubbles and pops until the recipe says to stop?

Is it burying one's head in the sand and staying quite motionless for forty-eight days until your brain hatches from the constant irritance of each grain?

Is it love? Romantic, erotic love that makes us an inherently shameless, insensitive, selfish people?

Is it pain or pleasure?

Is it distance?

Distance from each other and the world. A distance of three thousand miles could do—or so I've heard. Maybe one and a half if you're lucky. A score if you're not. Maybe it's cloying distances that plague us. Eats at my soul—breaks my heart—quarantines my lungs and limbs. Does distance reinvent human beings? Distance from a forgotten fascist past, or distance from an unrequited love. Distance from one's words or actions. Distance between friends.

Distanced from family.

If I think, therefore I am, then if I am, couldn't that just be another thought? An illusion? A holograph, or projection, or a PowerPoint presentation? Am I just living in Slides, with no transitions from one moment to another? A series of pictures in a flip book—and suddenly, I am whole at the end.

Am I part of some final plan, the Rapture, the End of the World? Do I play a part in it? If so, is it at least fun? Something comedic like Tevye or hopeless like Orpheus. Maybe I'm a Jet and my whole fate rides on whether or not Maria is actually pretty.

Or am I just a scribble on the Earth's surface?
What if I were the Earth?

Sometimes a scribble gets rid of all the bad ideas. The misspelt words and the laborious run-ons. I used to carry a notebook everywhere. Scribbling. Until one day, my brain and hand stopped working in tandem. My brain sprints but my hand sputters like an old motorcycle, whirring to life only in a classroom, under pressure. My brain is the hare, and my hand is the tortoise. In today's world, there's not much use for slow and steadfast. The fast and impulsive doesn't work either.

> **Now, it's impulsive and steadfast.**
> **The IRONMANs, not the 5Ks,**
> **that "Make It."**

I am a marathon, chugging along for four hours, making good time for a twenty-six-mile—two-hundred-year relay, a life extended onto me by my fore parents, my grandparents, my parents. A progression in the bloodline. Another awkward scribble. Here for a long time, not a fast life.

Sometimes, I want to stop.

> **I always want to stop.**

If I stopped, I worry I won't be able to restart that old motorcycle engine, and that I would feel all the oil leave my chassis, leaking onto the asphalt.

> **I need to keep going.**

That's my destiny.

Never stopping.

Never-ending.

Never living.

Until I **stop**.

XLIX

REGRET HANGOVER

—

WASHINGTON, 3 JULY 2020

She had noticed him first. Her heart dropped to her stomach even then, thumping. *Dhadam, dhadam.* He had been standing by the entrance near the fresh section. He was shaking out his wet baseball cap, before placing it back onto his head. A safe distance away. He had turned for only a split second, giving her just enough time to realize who he might be, before pivoting to the magazine rack. She had swallowed, and looked down at her gym clothes, retying her ponytail. He wouldn't recognize her; Nat was sure of it. Moving briskly to the pasta aisle, she started scanning her options.

"Here, have you tried this sauce?" Nat broke out of her thoughts, and this curly-haired stranger smiled at her gently.

"Sorry, what?" She cringed internally, and shifted her weight, maintaining a confident, albeit blushing, eye-contact. "Oh? This one? No, actually. Is it any good or just... primal?" Suddenly, her hand was in the shape of a claw in front of her face and she bemoaned her awkwardness.

A deep chuckle resonated from his chest, almost comically too dramatic. "Um... no, not exactly that kind of primal..." He trailed off into a lengthy description of his dietary habits and Nat found herself inadvertently checking him out. His long lashes, and the slight nervousness with which he stood, bouncing on his heels slightly. The light scar on his jawbone, hidden quite well by his stubble. "...Sorry... I just went vegan and can't help talking about it."

She snorted lightly and held in a full-blown laugh. He cocked his brow at the snort, and smirked. "Did you just snort?"

"Yeah. I'm not like other girls," Nat blurted. "But, you *are* vegan, so... I don't know which is worse."

After a beat, they both let out roaring belly laughs that went on for way longer than she had expected. "I'm sorry, that was kinda lame," she croaked with slightly teared up eyes. "I'm Natasha, by the way." Extending a hand, she was met with his name.

"Uh, it's Ben. Nice to meet you." He smiled down at her.

Nat felt some of the blood drain from her cheeks, and her heart thunder against her ribcage. *Black hair. Curly black hair, this has got to be a coincidence, right?! What?*

"Nice to meet you, too... Ben..." She subconsciously touched her phone and chewed on her lip. "So, you go to UVA...?"

Lazily, they made their way towards the regular checkout lane. She gestured for him to stand in front of her with a polite smile.

Anxiety filled the pit of her stomach, and she shifted her weight to her right leg. She didn't want to draw any more of his attention to her in the line and focused intently on reading the chocolate bar nutritional facts. She couldn't eat it, she knew that, but it gave her some time to kill.

Her eyes glazed over, as her attention shifted to a couple arguing outside by the entrance. Speaking of relationships, she made a mental note to text Omar. Pulling her phone out of her back pocket, she started typing out a message before realizing that she didn't have any service. *Crap, hopefully he's just parked outside. I am almost done.* Sighing, she shoved her phone out of sight and unsuccessfully tried to peer over this curly black-haired stranger's shoulder.

Catching a whiff of an unfamiliar cologne, Nat allowed herself to give the stranger a once-over. It *was* him. Ben. She could recognize the hair, the silhouette, the subtle hints. She noticed his phone, and his fingers as they darted and swiped across the darkly lit screen.

They hadn't met officially in person. In fact, they hadn't even seen each other properly. They hadn't even spoken about it. He was supposed to stay an enigma, an unknown variable. Instead, here he was in front of her, two feet away. Nat swallowed, visibly shaking slightly. She watched as his items were scanned, and he bagged them. She watched as he reached for the same chocolate bar she had been holding just moments earlier, as a smile passed over his lips, and as he set it down with his stuff. She knew he wouldn't recognize her. *Right?*

And even if he did, would he say anything? What if he'd just ignore her?

She started placing her items on the counter, trying to distract herself from his waiting body. *I think he's waiting for me.* The sinking feeling reached her toes, seeped into her clothes and made her breath quicken. She felt him move closer to her and clear his throat. She could almost feel his chest reverberate, and his hand gently touched the side of her arm. His cologne overpowered her, and she bit back a comment about Axe body-spray and middle school boys. It wasn't an offensive smell though, it was actually quite nice, and she didn't mind that he at least tried.

The heat of his stare never left her, however. As the items on the belt lessened, her heartbeat quickened.

One last ding broke their stare, when the cashier snapped at her. "Alright! That'll be $46.83, please. How would you like to pay?" The cashier lit up uncharacteristically positive.

"Uh... Card," she heard herself say, robotically moving closer to the bags and placing things inside her cart.

"Hey," his voice was surprisingly soft-spoken, kind. "Do I know you? You just seem really familiar..."

Forced to meet his gaze, she jutted her chin out and raised a brow. "I'm sorry, I—I don't think so." Before she could complete her sentence, faint recognition dawned on his face. His five o'clock shadow looked better in person, she observed unhelpfully, and even under the cap his curls knotted at the base of his neck and around his forehead. Breathtaking. Here he was, in front of her, a real person.

The world stopped.

He kept staring until the last protein shake was in her tote, and she gave the cashier a hurried smile without taking her receipt.

Anxiously, she bolted through the doors, and felt a splatter of water pelt her. *Fuck*, she groaned. Sheepishly, Nat pulled her cart under the scaffold, and pulled off her scrunchie, shaking out her drenched hair. She felt a little calmer in the fresh air. The viscous scent of wet asphalt comforted her, as she gathered herself. *It was too hot inside, anyway. They must have turned the heater up all the way or... something.* She slowly inhaled, focusing on the rapidly moistening asphalt, and sighed. She couldn't see Omar outside, and Nat groaned inwardly. He usually parked in the overflow lot, a five-minute walk away. And, in this downpour, suddenly she felt too tired to make it to his car. *Why was he here? Wasn't he living with his—*

The door shuddered open, and she darted closer to the wall, trying to hide her frame. A young mother-son pair, shielded by a large umbrella, walked briskly towards their car. Nat sighed, and felt the exposed brick scrape her back; she leaned back on the wall and shut her eyes, trying to slow her breath, reprimand her heart. Sucking her teeth, she grabbed onto her hair and retied it with determination. She had to walk in the rain, she was bound to get wet by the time she reached the overflow lot, and she had no choice but to start now. Sooner rather than later, right?

The door opened again, and *he* stepped out. She blanched, a wave of nausea hitting her all of a sudden. Nat pretended to busy herself with her bags and pulled out her phone. A shadow fell over her silhouette as Ben moved towards her.

After a short, pregnant pause, he cleared his throat. "Are you in the other lot?"

Chewing on her lip, she spoke quietly. "Yeah. I am."

"Do you want to walk together?"

The rain continued to pour, pelting them with soft, pillowy droplets. It was a welcome change after the dry heat of the summer months. A welcome change before the air froze and the sun hid behind clouds. They shared a few shy glances. Nat's bags were swinging violently by her side as she tried to keep up with his long strides. He slowed down every few steps, looking over at her cautiously.

"I…" He started lamely. Nat cringed internally, and she noticed his jaw lock just slightly as he turned towards her. "We do know each other though?"

"Sure, yeah… I guess. I dunno, peripherally, maybe. I have a couple friends at UVA. But, I've like never visited or anything." *Peripherally? What kind of prick uses the word peripherally?!* Nat bit her tongue for barely a moment before quickly saying. "I mean. I think we know each other. Maybe just not our faces." *And, why the fuck did I say that?* She pretended not to notice his knee-jerk reaction to check her out, slowing down as he did. *He knows.*

"Honestly, I don't think I'd forget you." Ben grinned sheepishly, giving her a long sideways glance. Her breath caught, and she gulped inadvertently, nearly stopping. *Why am I so nervous?* Helpfully, he offered his hand, gesturing at her wet and heavy bags. "I don't mind helping with those."

For a moment, it felt completely normal that this stranger, materializing from her phone and in front of her, was also her first lover. *Ben.* His name sounded foreign to her ears, and even more foreign to her tongue. The syllables twisted and contorted uncomfortably.

"So," He chuckled. "The bags?" With a small half-smile, she nodded and handed one of them to him.

"Thanks," she replied. "I usually don't park so far away."

"And, I usually don't help strangers with their grocery bags."

Nat smirked, stifling a laugh. "Yeah? This must be doing wonders for your karmic balances, then." He looked like a lost puppy for a millisecond and she nearly melted.

"Okay… I meant it, by the way. I think we've met before. You seem super familiar."

"I really don't think we've met, to be honest."

"Well, we have now!"

"Okay, true…" Nat grinned lopsidedly. Her phone buzzed familiarly, three rapid vibrations. *That's* his *tone,* she thought confusedly. *But, he isn't texting…* She snuck a glance at him, with her bag in one hand and his in another. *So… this is just a fluke. A coincidence.* "One sec. I think my, uh, friend just texted me!"

Pausing, she checked her messages, finding a new one from her first lover. *Ben.* A wave of relief washed over her as the rain started showing signs of slowing down. The man next to her and the man behind the screen were not the same person. Two different people, two doppelgängers, one unfortunate run-in.

As more droplets pelted down, they joked and finally made their way to Omar's waiting car. The lights were on, and she could hear his playlist blaring over the rain's noise.

"Nat! Natasha!" Omar rapped on the window and cracked it open only slightly. "What the hell, *yaar?* Why did you take so long?!"

"Sorry, sorry. Ran into a friend." She gestured awkwardly at Ben with the bags and nodded towards the trunk. "Since you're not going to get out," she grimaced, "can you at least open the trunk?"

Omar rolled his eyes and rolled up the window. The trunk beeped and the two of them made their way behind the car.

"Uh... Is that your... brother?" Ben asked, innocently, as he helped her load the bags into the car.

"Hm... not exact—no. No, he's a friend." Nat replied sheepishly, furrowing her eyebrows. "He's going back to India tomorrow so I'm treating him to dinner."

"Oh. Okay."

"Not like that," she rushed out. "I'm not *with* him or anything. Just a friend."

Ben nodded thoughtfully and turned to face her. The trunk was still open, providing them with a cover from the rain and a gust of hot air from the car. "In that case, can I maybe get your number, or do you have Snap?"

Nat blanched ever so slightly, before a rush of color flooded her cheeks. Magenta. "Uh... I don't have Snap. Phone's good. Yeah, that's—sure." She lied. *Well, it was a half-truth, she* had *made a Snap for Ben. The* other *Ben.*

"I'm only in town for the long weekend, but if you're free..." Nat chuckled and nodded, reciting her phone number. "Awesome! I'll see you around, then?"

"Yup, see you around!"

Nat shut the trunk and watched as Ben walked to his car. He turned and gave her a slight wave, before readjusting his baseball cap. Tearing her eyes away from him, she realized how soaked she had become standing in the rain. Rushing towards the passenger's side, Nat sat down and grimaced when feeling the wetness of her clothes squelch on the faux leather. "Sorry, Om. I know this is a rental."

"It's okay, dude," Omar grinned. "Though you have to make up for it!"

Rolling her eyes, Nat groaned. "I'm literally making you dinner, asshole. Nothing more's coming out of this, remember?"

"Hey, I never said anything about coming." He chuckled as he started the car and buckled up, while Nat followed suit. He glanced over at her to make sure she was ready to go. She nodded with a small smile and let down her hair.

Pulling out her phone, she typed in the address to the extended stay hotel Omar was at and let it connect to the car's system. "Here, I punched in the address." Nat looked over at him. "Can't believe you're leaving tomorrow, dude." Turning back to her phone, she started typing out a message to Rumi.

Omar grunted, and she saw him increase the volume of the music. Nat leaned back into the seat and realized that she hadn't gotten Ben's number. He just had hers. *Hm, I guess it'll be up to him to make the first move, huh?*

What she didn't notice was the message from Ben, sitting neatly unread in her **The Chatroom** inbox. A message that had arrived nearly five minutes ago. She didn't notice that her phone had just reconnected with the internet. That Ben's profile picture was a Wahoo, the mascot from UVA. That he had been on his phone, too, swiping and grinning stupidly at her last message. A joke about shopping at Whole Foods. That he had replied with "I'm literally at Whole Foods rn."

L

ANTH

——

We all live different versions of the same life.

A collective twenty-first century American teenage experience. It's all more or less the same. Bedrooms, phones, lazy weekends, and exhausting weekdays. Ennui: presumably, due to a lack of purpose. Longing for silver screened romances and abusive fanfiction boyfriends. Y/N and roguish smiles from K-Pop stars. Gifs of TV psychopaths and vampires smirking or biting their lips. Tumblr smut.

All the boys I've ever loved have treated me badly. I don't know if it's because I've come to not expect anything more than their attention or teeny, tiny slivers of their time or if it's because girls have been socialized to believe they're not supposed to be treated as equals all the time. So, that bleeds into our conceptions of love and romance. Is it archaic to think that? Am I just being naive, or worse heteronormative, when I say all women have a tendency to do this?

A girl's time is just as valuable as a man's or a boy's. In fact, time is important to everyone.

Time is a privilege. I can just sit around for two days in a week, because I don't have people to take care of. I don't have a household to run. I'm still a child in so many ways, even if I've been mentally prepared to find a mate for a decade. I think *that man* broke him a little, a lot that night. I wasn't supposed to feel so ashamed, so sick to my stomach, after sending my first nude. I felt gross. But, the first time I sent a picture to Ben, I was excited.

Time determines everything.

If I were in a room with all the boys I've ever loved, I wouldn't want to be in that room. I'd be uncomfortable and nauseous. Disgusted by my standards in men and repulsed by the fact that they're probably still assholes. Years later, they probably are the same inherent type of person: a jerk. And worse, if my type hasn't evolved from messy, hormonal jerk to… something less volatile, what does that say about me? I wouldn't want to run into any of their arms because, quite honestly, they never deserved my love. All *they* had to do was just exist, and I loved them unconditionally, expecting nothing back and believing that was healthy.

Don't get me wrong. Unconditional love is also extremely beautiful and necessary for the human race to propagate (what isn't as unconditional as a parent's love for their child?) But, is it always good for a romantic love to be… unconditional? To not expect *anything,* including kindness or respect or acknowledgment.

I have loved these boys unconditionally because I was never *with* them. I didn't spend time with them, sneak out of my house to see them, drive to stranded parking lots to make out with them, or watch their games to cheer them on. I didn't actually participate in any of their lives. I didn't exist in their universe. Ever. I just saw them, and liked them, and allowed that teeny morsel of physical appreciation to grow into something more. I didn't force it on them, but I wasn't shy about it… Just stupid. I can still remember some of the highlights with them.

Like that one time, I caught his eye in class, and Ryan saw me looking at him. The sun was streaming through the windows, casting shadows over our desks. I didn't think he'd notice me looking, and his blue eyes were looking bluer than ever. I didn't realize the light was hitting me, too. So, he saw me. And my breath caught, and my heart jumped, and my stomach dropped, and a surge of oxytocin overtook my body, and I stared. Then, when he slipped me an earth-shattering smile and I was red-cheeked and slack-jawed, I knew I loved Ryan.

I just, in the pit of my stomach, knew that I wanted to be with him so fucking much.

Did it distract me from school? No.

Did it reorganize my priorities? Of course not.

Did it give me something sweet to look forward to at the start of every day? Yeah, a little bit.

He broke my heart so early that as a teenager, I realized I didn't want to spend my years wiling away with someone.

But, I wiled away with Ben. Every text, every Snap, every stupid second I read the words "is typing…" I wiled away with him. And I loosened up in more ways than one. I became more open to the idea of him chasing me and meeting at some predetermined location and time. Or calling him and finally hearing his voice. Thinking about him, dreaming about him, became too natural. Maybe it's because he's so far away, I didn't think it would ever happen. But, maybe it's because he's so far away, that the desi-movie-loving hopeless romantic in me wanted it to happen. Wanted him to fly three-thousand miles, call me with his phone number and speak through unmistaken excitement and anticipation.

But that's not what'll happen. That was never a timeline. That never existed in the billions of parallel universes, one where we both fell in love together at the same time doesn't exist. But I'll keep thinking about him almost as though we do live in that spectacular, idealized timeline. The one where we're married and living above a Chinese restaurant in New York.

Why did Ben reorganize my priorities? Why do I think about him so much? Is it because I have too much time on my hands? Is that what grown-up love is supposed to be? Where I make space for the other person in my heart? Clean out a drawer and some closet space, so they can move in for a few weeks?

I feel like every time my heart gets broken it just congeals into one mass again over the course of a few months. But it's inherently fucked up. Like some arteries aren't where they need to be, and eventually a doctor, as they peer over my body on an operating table, will declare I need a triple-bypass due to a love failure. Open-heart surgery will tell me how fucked up my feelings are for all the boys I've ever loved. And how will I know I've broken my heart again? I can barely feel love anymore. Even the kind of love I know—I *know*—I have for Rumi, or my parents, or grandparents. The love I know, for a fact, I *don't* have for myself.

Maybe, that's the problem. I don't love myself, so I'm looking for love from others.

Unreliable, stupid others. Others like Omar, who once drunkenly threatened to drive to my house in the middle of the night and bang on the front door, asking my shocked parents for my hand in matrimony—like some discount Devdas. Like, what the fuck even is that?

Others like Ben.

Sweet, dumb Ben. Who could never handle me in real life but had the audacity to tell me to fuck off via text. The asshole that wasted my time and my emotions and my nudes. The asshole who will just leave, without having the decency to say bye… or to unblock me. The asshole who will manage to make me feel winded from three-thousand miles away:

Ben.

I'm looking forward to it; after all, after Ben breaks my heart, who else do I turn to? I can't spend any more tears on him. I already cried the night I accidentally confessed to Omar that I loved *him*—Ben. I couldn't even look Omar in the eyes or speak to him for a solid half-hour. He just held me as I cried, and I didn't know if I wanted to thank him or curse him out for trying to fuck me an hour later.

Rumi? No, she doesn't need my emotional baggage in her life right now. Or ever. We've spent too many nights talking about guys. It's time to move on from the transients from our lives and move toward each other. When we were in high school, we would spend hours ruminating the meaning of life, and our purpose in the future. When did we become so boring, so obviously one-dimensional in our relationship? I love this girl to death, and I don't want her to become my emotional crutch. That's not at all respectful to our friendship. Plus, I have to learn to deal with myself. I don't know how to. I am a self-encompassed human being, or as Modi would say, *atmanirbhar.*

Mummy? Daddy? They've never really had their hearts broken. I think. Honestly, I'm not too sure… maybe they have, over some forgotten adolescent crush or film star, but never in a relationship. I don't know what to ask them. I don't want to ask them. I don't want to shatter the only pristine image of love I have.

I don't have anyone to rely on but myself here. These are my emotions to fight against. Or fight with. I don't know which emotions are good for me.

Ben's just gone. He's poofed. He's Houdini-ed. He's vanished, and I'll never know him. And, he will never have the chance to actually know who I am and what I could have been for him. I want to throw up. I want to just shout at traffic, or drive to Canada on a whim. I don't know if I want to fight or flee.

I can't think clearly, and all I want to do is smile and hold back my tears. Even as they roll down my cheeks, I want to hold them back. I don't want to cry for him. I can't help but cry for him. I don't know if I'm crying for him or for myself. I don't want tonight to end. I don't want tonight to end. I want to keep feeling this pain, because if I wake up in the morning, and I don't feel anything—

Then I know for a fact, he was never anyone to me.

Just another phantom I could name, rather than dream of. Whose curly black hair will follow me to sleep, whose arms and typos will forever haunt me. I feel so stupid. So cheated, and so… heart broken.

Anthim sanskar: the Hindu final rites. That's what this feels like.

Anthim means final.

Anth means end.

The final rites to our relationship and my feelings for him. In the coming months, I know I'll feel a lot more. Every once in a while, some morsel of emotion or sadness or despair will pop out, and I'll have to remember again. Remember… nothing. We never had memories or fun times or dates or kisses or moments that we both knew were special. We just had words on a terminal screen that, well, are stored in a server somewhere. Probably somewhere cold and Scandinavian, close to where Lisbeth Salander lives. And, I'm supposed to mourn him. I guess, our relationship.

Breakups are always messy. But, was this even a breakup? Did Ben even exist in the way I thought he did? Did he actually ever send me his favorite songs or his homework problems? Did I ever make him smile or stay up way past dawn? Did I crowd his thoughts like he did mine? Is he entitled to the same kinds of feelings I have right now? Was I in love with him or did I just love him? Did I love him because he made me like myself a little bit? Because he softened my edges and made me feel sexy? Will I ever be able to feel sexy without him or another… boy?

Ben isn't dead. He ghosted. And when I specifically asked him not to. Thrice. Three times in our chats, three times I told him it would suck butt if he left me on read one day. I hadn't even considered him blocking me. At least I still kind of trust him… Unless I find my nudes on some Russian revenge porn site. That'd be momentous. Maybe a bit nauseating, but honestly, who'd want to actually see my pictures?

Did he miraculously find a girlfriend? Is that what happened? Two days since our last exchange, and he's shacked up and cuffed?

Was I his side hoe? Cause I literally cannot even fuck with that. I am so fucking over it. How the fuck did *he* find someone? That is not, in his words, a "thot." In a fucking quarantine. What.

And, as any rational human being would while spiraling, I started looking for my rebound. I started looking for other people to fill his void in stupid, superfluous ways. Someone else to tell me a week in that they miss talking to me when we're not actively texting or that they want to play with my hair. Or that they want to bend me over.

Every day will pass, business as usual, as it was before Ben. And, after Ryan. And, after Omar. And, after another one. And, another someone.

It's October again, and another year has just whizzed by me. A year full of firsts and lasts, I suppose. I guess I should be thankful I'm not in my dorm again, crying to old Indian love songs, and imagining fake relationships with faceless strangers. I shouldn't be as gleeful about the global circum-stances that have determined this moment for me. I'm home, finally. A home I was able to reclaim after some time away. And, I'm not even picking up the pieces of my relationship or my heart. In any case, even though Omar left in July and I'm back to being sexually frustrated 24/7, I'm kind of glad he isn't here. He always made me feel lacking in some way, whether it was because of my weight, or my goals, or my age. I've learned to validate myself, because I've given up on ever feeling truly valid.

Until one day, maybe just one day, I'll meet someone who doesn't fuck off after three months—and that person will be the person I always hoped to see in the reflection of my mirror.

Until I finally meet the Nat—the *Natasha*—who has ownership and finds her purpose and takes charge of her life and graduates school *summa cum laude* and lives in LA and drives an Audi and somehow has a social life on top of all her responsibilities. I don't even want to think about the infinite number of Ryans or Bens I could possibly meet.

Until she meets me.

AFTERWORD

I live to read.

My first love is and will always be books. Ever since I was a child, I've been telling stories, listening to stories, and reading and re-reading my favorite ones in yellowed, dog-eared copies.

My love for reading transcended online quickly after I moved to the United States in 2009. I read Wikipedia article after Wikipedia article, scanned lists of the highest-grossing films, and… More books. Well, fanfiction and online chick-lit on Wattpad. Reading a lot of fanfiction, which most people dismiss as a silly teenage girl endeavor, I voraciously consumed words as a young, impressionable tween. I fell in love with the idea of love then. Meet-cutes, sweet nothings, pushing hair behind Y/N's ear.

I've fallen in love, too. A lot. With people I know, people I'm friends with, people I barely know, people I've never spoken to… For me, love is an easily expendable emotion. According to my mum, it's very easy to fall in love with a lot of people, maybe even simultaneously. I think my high school classmates would second that opinion about me. I've never been selfish about romantic love, but I will admit to being picky with platonic love.

But, most controversially, at age fifteen I'd fallen in love with strangers whom I'd only texted. If that doesn't seem like the most bizarre thing you've read in a while, I wouldn't be surprised. Scrolling through some revealing social media posts referring to the collective Gen Z experience, I started to realize that chat-room culture has existed for a while and many similarly aged people have had problematic, exploitative encounters online.

Teenagers (and, tweenagers) interact with online predators more frequently now but in more insidious ways since overt predatory interactions are less common; as CNN reports, "unwanted sexual solicitations [of children] declined 53 percent between 2000 and 2010."[7]

Shows with disturbing titles like *Catfish*, *To Catch a Predator*, and *Dateline* exemplify how people can never be trusted but are vestiges of the late 1990s and early 2000s. It doesn't help that all around the world many children under the age of thirteen already have access to a screen and a stable internet connection. Underage TikTok stars and Instagram influencers exacerbate an already volatile situation.

Seeing as these influencers are minors, I feel as though it would be inappropriate and irresponsible to call them out so blatantly, especially since they have been so vastly sexualized in their careers and their guardians do not act as buffers between them and the rest of the world. Hence, the world is inundated with free, accessible images of young, impressionable children doing precocious, problematic things on a public stage as well as unnecessarily sharing parts of their personal lives. This leads to something more sinister and

---

7   Christine Elgersma, "Parents, Here's the Truth about Online Predators." *Cable News Network*, August 3, 2017.

coercive even between two young consenting adults, known as sextortion, or "the *threat* to expose a sexual image to coerce the victim into doing something, even if exposure of the image never actually occurs."[8]

This is a dramatic shift from copies of *Lolita* being banned in 1960s America. On the flip side, students are also a lot more aware to what predatory behavior may look like; schools discuss cyber-safety, promote anti-cyber-bullying campaigns, and first- and second-hand experiences help with a young person's understanding of online threats. After all, we live in an age of swiping and social media. Instagram, Twitter, and even to some extent Facebook and Myspace, changed the dating game for most people. My uncle and aunt met online in the early 2000s. When Indian matrimonial sites moved online by the 2010s, another uncle was able to meet his future wife.

At fifteen, I felt a lot older than I really was. I think we all did or do. Even Taylor Swift did and wrote a song about it! When I look at pictures or selfies from that year, I see a fresh-faced innocence (that I believe I still possess in some ways) that I nearly radiated. Sophomore year in high school you feel older because you're not just starting high school, but actually taking harder classes and having some ownership of your space. People pay more attention to you, and you start your journey of self-determination. At least I did.

Nat hasn't grown out of her young adulthood—maybe, as far as authors like to do with their fictional characters, I want to believe she may never grow out of this. Even at nineteen, Natasha is and will always be the quintessential teenager.

---

8   Janis Wolak et al., "Sextortion of Minors: Characteristics and Dynamics," *Journal of Adolescent Health* 62, no. 1 (2018): 73.

Ants is a book that is entirely grounded in the temporality and real-life events of the year 2020. Thank you for reliving this year with Natasha and me in a small way. You witnessed her journey of finding love after a chance online encounter. On a day that seemed like many other days, Nat meets Ben, another lonely touch-hungry teen three thousand miles away. Nat doesn't know how she feels about this boy, but with her penchant to fantasize, she creates elaborate scenarios starting and ending their relationship. All of this while never seeing his face, hearing his voice, or holding his hand. She doesn't know fully how real he is, but that doesn't stop her from imagining.

Love transcends a lot of physical and societal separators already: race, age, socioeconomic background, caste (in India's case), religion. But, can someone truly fall in love with a person they've never seen or met? In this world, isn't the first impression incredibly important in informing the subconscious mind of our feelings for a person?

As mainstream as online dating has become, stranger danger still persists, and for a good reason, too! The stereotype of Indian men online sliding into the direct messages of young, or even foreign, women, *Dirty John,* and horror stories of Craigslist meetups gone wrong exist simultaneously in a cyberspace full of fast, casual dating like Tinder.

But, as naïve as it may sound, I believe in the inherent goodness of people all around the world. Individuals look out for each other when society doesn't; in the case of Rahul Dubey, looking out for his community meant helping safeguard Black Lives Matter protesters from the police in June 2020.[9] And, even with stranger danger in the back of my

---

9   Mariya Moseley, "The Quiet Army Supporting Black Lives Matter Protests." *ABC News Network,* June 14, 2020.

mind, the heart does what it wants — and I've fallen in love, facelessly, namelessly, dangerously.

I wrote *Ants* because I am Natasha.

In fact, I believe there is a bit of Nat in everybody. Whether it's because you've felt displaced, aimless, lost at love, despaired in heartbreak, found love online, found love offline, are a fan of hookup culture, are a fan of the idea of love at first sight, have experienced unrequited love, moved continents, failed achieving at your goals, you will find something here.

For example, Natasha's South Asian heritage makes her accessible to the few hundred million urban South Asians, living in a subcontinent thousands of miles away; yet her foreignness also makes her inaccessible for many of the three-hundred million Americans. Through the well-intentioned reasoning of five-thousand-year-old Hindu priests and gods, Nat has experienced the dichotomy of Indian gender norms. Shakti, the goddess of strength, rides a tiger, holding a *trishūl* (trident) and devours her enemies. Yet Delhi, the political capital of India, is also known as the rape capital of the country. Goddesses are feared and revered, while women aren't allowed to show their faces in the princely state of Rajasthan in northwestern India. Nat and I both have the privilege of growing up in extremely progressive Indian households, unlike millions of other South Asian women. Living as a hyphenated American fundamentally challenges people to conceal or disguise parts of their culture and code-switch, which is to use different words and mannerisms around specific groups of people. Perhaps, you might have felt uncomfortable or confused while reading "Dakshina"—that is only a fraction of what so many immigrants, non-English speakers, and the like feel in a country as vast and culturally homogenous as the United States. It's

an experience I, a native English speaker, was forced to have
when I moved to this country; an experience my parents,
also native English speakers, had while attempting to code-
switch in public spaces, on the phone, or at work. My words
didn't—and still don't really—fit in the American lexicon.
They're peppered with mispronunciations, awkward pauses,
an American accent that doesn't work all the time, and the
occasional adoption of the Canadian 'SO-ree' rather than
the American 'SAW-ree.'

Nat, like many hyphenated Americans, will never fit into
the hegemony of a white, middle-class patriarchal America.
That isn't as much of a debate as it is a cold, hard fact. In fact,
I use the term South Asian rather than Asian because Americans perceive Asians as East Asians rather than the other
thousands of ethnic groups from the Asian continent. It is
the intersectionality of Nat's experiences and worldview that
make her unique, yet part of several communities all over the
globe. It is the same intersectionality that every individual
has that goes into shaping their identity.

Therefore, Nat does not have a universal experience; but
when do we ever read a book to re-imagine a life we already
know or the life we have?

Fictional as *Ants* is, I realized the experience of this year
has been so unique to the majority of the world that I could
not just discount the global pandemic, the resurgence of civil
rights activism in the United States, the rise of democratical-
ly-elected despots, the terrifying realization of the climate
crisis (as a member of Gen Z), and all the other things that
seem to be debilitatingly wrong in the world. While this book
cannot address all these topics, the feeling of despondency—a lethargic depression—is recreated in Nat's pathology.
It is also a reminder of Nat's obvious, unspoken privilege.

As I write this, I am overwhelmed by my own feelings of melancholy for a childhood I can never revisit. Nat's journey, as you might have noticed, is rooted in her sense of displacement after leaving her parents' home for college; she seeks validation from the world because she doesn't feel at home anymore. So many students experience this ill-defined moment between childhood and adulthood that we like to call adolescence or the teenage experience.

Every single teenager I know has multiple, developed facades for each community they interact with on a regular basis. Many teens are forced to dress, speak, and act differently in school as opposed to their non-educational environments. I'm one of the few children of immigrants, and children in general, who feels completely at ease swearing in front of her parents. This wasn't an overnight switch as much as it was a slow, determined marathon to be able to express myself freely in front of them. Teenagers are stuck in a rut between perceived maturity after their eighteenth birthdays and their childhoods — while they would hate going back in time or back to middle-school, they love reminiscing about their Fruit Loops and PBS Kids days.

Characters aren't meant to symbolize the realest of humans; there's always a flair of unexpected behavior and volatility that most humans like to keep hidden.

As one of those kinds of humans, I enjoyed writing Nat very much. She represents the duplicity and duality of the teenage experience — sneaking away in her *petites rebellions* online while passing as an average, highly-ambitious desi teenager — while also attempting to embody an entirely feminine ideal. And, like all characters, Nat is a hollow creation of my mind – she is not a real person and hasn't lived a full life. She is a mask for you, dear reader, to consider wearing for a few hours: seeing the world through her eyes and living in her mind.

I urge you to keep reading about Nat's story because, unique romance angle aside, it describes the growing tension between how older generations and the newer generations view commitment, monogamy, and love. Nat is confused all the time, and maybe it was tragic, frustrating, or shocking for you to read. Let it be confusing and frustrating. Nat is emotional, vulnerable, and hurting. She deserves to have her story told, because, as hundreds of comments on social media have revealed, it isn't a unique experience. Meeting one's partner online is more commonplace than ever, but as an impressionable young adult, is it really the right place to court strangers?

Or even more importantly, is it the best place for predators to find their prey? And if so, who in Nat's story is the prey?

APPENDIX

—

XI. ARUNDHATI-VASISHTHA

Narayan, M.K.V. *Flipside of Hindu Symbolism: Sociological and Scientific Linkages in Hinduism.* Fultus Books, 2007.

XIII. CITY OF STARS

Chazelle, Damien, dir. *La La Land.* 2015; Los Angeles, CA: Warner Bros. Pictures, 2016.

Fitzgerald, F. Scott. *The Great Gatsby.* New York: Charles Scribner's Sons, 1925.

Wilder, Billy, dir. *Sunset Boulevard.* 1950; Los Angeles: Paramount Pictures, 1950.

XXXVIII. TAILSPIN

Imani, Sayyid Kamal Faqhih. "Section 14: Surah Al-Baqarah, Verses 116-117." In *An Enlightening Commentary into the Light*

of the Holy Qur'an vol. 1, translated by Sayyid Abbas Sadr-
'ameli, 194–196. Imam Ali Foundation.

"Kun Faya Kun Full Video Song Rockstar | Ranbir Kapoor | A.R.
Rahman, Javed Ali, Mohit Chauhan." Posted on December
5, 2011, YouTube video, 6:20. https://youtu.be/T94PHkuydcw.

AFTERWORD

Elgersma, Christine. "Parents, Here's the Truth about Online Predators." CNN. *Cable News Network*, August 3, 2017. https://www.
cnn.com/2017/08/03/health/online-predators-parents-partner/
index.html.

Moseley, Mariya. "The Quiet Army Supporting Black Lives Matter Protests." ABC. *ABC News Network*, June 14, 2020. https://
abcnews.go.com/US/quiet-army-supporting-black-lives-mat-
ter-protests/story?id=71142168.

Wolak, Janis, and David Finkelhor. "Sextortion of Minors: Characteristics and Dynamics," *Journal of Adolescent Health* 62, no.
1 (2018): 72–79. https://doi.org/10.1016/j.jadohealth.2017.08.014.

www.ingramcontent.com/pod-product-compliance
Lightning Source LLC
Chambersburg PA
CBHW051439050726
47593CB00005B/1842